UNDERDOGS AND TRICKSTERS

NEW VOICES IN BIBLICAL STUDIES
Edited by John J. Collins
OTHER TITLES IN THE SERIES:

UNDERDOGS AND TRICKSTERS

A Prelude to Biblical Folklore

SUSAN NIDITCH

1817

Harper & Row, Publishers, San Francisco

Cambridge, Hagerstown, New York, Philadelphia, Washington
London, Mexico City, São Paulo, Singapore, Sydney

FIRST EDITION

Library of Congress Cataloging-in-Publication Data

Niditch, Susan.
    Underdogs and tricksters.

    (New voices in biblical studies)
    Bibliography: p.
    Includes index.
    1. Folklore in the Bible.   I. Title.   II. Series.
BS625.N53   1987   221.8'398352   86-46209
ISBN 0-06-254605-8

87 88 89 90 91 RRD 10 9 8 7 6 5 4 3 2 1

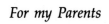

For my Parents

Contents

Acknowledgments

This book was written with the help of a grant from the National Endowment for the Humanities. I thank those who have taken an interest in my work, serving as referees for grant proposals, offering helpful bibliographic information, posing good questions, and providing encouragement: John Collins, Robert Oden, Edgar Slotkin, George Coats, Robert Wilson, Robert Culley, Burke Long, John Kselman, Barbara Kirshenblatt-Gimblett, David Bynum, Veena Das, and Dan Ben-Amos. Special thanks go to John Collins, who first suggested I write a book on folklore and the Bible. He read the manuscript with great care and, together with George Lawler, helped enormously in the revision process. The manuscript was also read by Albert Lord, who offered thoughtful suggestions and gentle criticism. I thank him and Frank Moore Cross for their help and teaching over the years.

A grant from Amherst College aided in preparation of the manuscript. I thank Diane Beck for her fine work in typing the manuscript and Derek Krueger for preparing the Index with care and caring. Finally, I thank my husband, Robert Doran, who participates in important ways in all my projects, and our little bird, Rebecca Doran, who loves the stories of Genesis as much as anyone I know.

Introduction

The Corpus and the Methodology

The Hebrew Bible is rich in underdog tales. The underdog is the poor relative, the youngest son, the exile, the ex-prince, the soldier of a defeated army—the person, in short, who is least likely to succeed and yet does. The underdog evokes our sympathies; we root for underdogs because of the underdog aspect of our lives, our insecurities real or imagined, and when they succeed we succeed. Underdogs make their way through native wisdom or physical prowess, often with the help of an agent, human or divine, and figure prominently in various folk narrative traditions.

The trickster is a subtype of the underdog. A fascinating and universal folk hero, the trickster brings about change in a situation via trickery. Although biblical tricksters are a much more sedate version of the character type than the bawdy examples of West African mythology, they display some of the same ambiguities in motivation and realization of goals. They never gain full control of the situation around them and often escape difficulties in a less than noble way. Their tale does not end with unequivocal success, but they survive to trick again—and, indeed, are survivors par excellence. Trickster narratives help us to cope with the insurmountable and uncontrollable forces in our own lives, personifying and in a sense containing the chaos that always threatens.

The underdog and the trickster are traditional characters in a broad, cross-cultural literary corpus. I believe, however, that they held special appeal for the Israelite composers who shaped the tales of their ancestral heroes; for throughout its history, Israel has had a peculiar self-image as the underdog and the trickster.

Claiming rights to a land miles from its roots in Mesopotamia, having as its major historical leitmotifs themes of enslavement and escape, exile and restoration, conscious of its origins as a mixed multitude, and self-conscious about its affinities with Canaanite culture, Israel produced narratives that ultimately served to shore up group identity and self-esteem, that emphasized independence from and superiority over hostile enemies, and that proclaimed Israelite uniqueness. The stories of Israelite heroes not only reflect the community that is Israel but, indeed, helped to form it.

This study explores a variety of biblical tales about underdogs and tricksters: three variants of the same narrative, the wife-sister tales of Genesis 12:10–20; 20:1–18; and 26:1–17; two tale cycles about successful younger sons, Jacob (Gen. 25–36) and Joseph (Gen. 37–50); and an interesting tale that combines in unique ways a variety of traditional folk motifs and themes, the Book of Esther.

My study of these tales is informed by a particular methodological focus. I seek to introduce, explore, and apply the cross-discipline that is folklore. Not since Hermann Gunkel, who was deeply immersed in folkloristics as it was understood in his time, has this field been adequately reassessed or its methods systematically applied to the literature of the Hebrew Scriptures. For Gunkel, folklore studies consisted of two major tasks: the collection of literature by scholars (such as Jacob and Wilhelm Grimm) so that a good sampling of folklore became available for comparative literary purposes and the preliminary cataloguing of the sorts of folklore that existed, the early folklorist's equivalent to form-criticism.

The field of folklore studies has, of course, grown and evolved over the years, and Bible scholars have much catching up to do in folklore scholarship, but Gunkel's careful attention to the relevance of folk literature to biblical literature remains worthy of emulation. Though a work such as Robert Alter's *The Art of Biblical Narrative* shows enormous literary sensitivity to the textures of biblical narrative, comparisons with Flaubert or Kafka may not be as helpful as comparisons with folktale material. Gunkel, early in the history of modern scholarship, understood that biblical literature is ultimately traditional literature.

Biblical Literature As Traditional Literature

Biblical literature, is traditional literature having more in common with Homer's *Odyssey* than a Faulkner novel, with a Child ballad than a Robert Lowell poem, with a Zande ritual drama than a Sam Shepard play. To describe biblical literature as traditional is to notice its repeated patterns of thought, content, and language, traceable to no single originator, recurring within individual works, in different works of the same period, and in works of varying periods. It is to speak of cultural and literary assumptions shared by composers and intended audiences, participants in the biblical process. To speak of traditional style is not necessarily to seek origins for much of biblical literature in oral literature, that is, literature composed by authors trained to create their songs or tales in live performance without the aid of writing.[1] Hints of such roots may be suggested by the language and literary forms of some biblical works, but searches for the oral history of biblical literature are often intriguing wild goose chases. What we can say with certainty is that in the Hebrew Scriptures there are ways to report an appearance of God, to berate an unfaithful people, or to narrate the life history of an unlikely hero. There are modes of speech, means of expression, natural to authors and expected by audiences, pieces of content that rightly belong in such reports or tales. One should not envision a rigid adherence to conventions, for fresh and flexible improvisation within traditional forms is at the heart of all folklore, including orally composed works[2]—considered by many the most "traditional" of traditional-style works.[3] Nontraditional composers also share conventions, being products of cultural milieux beyond themselves or their own literary circles, but culturally shared patterning is more apparent in traditional literature and lore than in nontraditional creations, the preference for old means of expression over new ones more consistent,[4] the web of interlocking relations between compositions by different authors more pervasive.

Not all Old Testament literature is equally traditional in these ways. The Book of Ruth, for example, might be described as a less traditional, more individualistic story than Genesis 41, which has variants in Daniel and corresponds to a universal folktale type. Ruth's ordinary people contrast with Genesis 41's archetypal king, helpless local magicians, and wise foreigner.[5] If we can agree, however, that much of biblical literature is traditional-style literature, then it becomes clear that students of Scripture have much to learn from the professional students of traditional lore and literature, folklorists.

Defining the Field

Defining the field of folklore has long been a concern of folklorists themselves.[6] Some limit their field of study to pieces of literature demonstrably composed and transmitted orally at some point in their history: for example, Homer's *Odyssey*, the ballads of the Child collection, or the epics of the Milman Parry collection.[7] Other folklorists (probably most these days) include various aspects of folk life such as folk dance, weaving and quilting, water-divining, and occupational speech patterns. Others would include typologically describable examples of popular culture, such as the scripts of situation comedies or the plots of horror movies. Some would consider true "folklore" to be only performed works, lore in process,[8] "in its indigenous set of live contexts."[9] For these scholars, the *Odyssey* and the creations preserved in the Bible that are the focus of our study in this book exemplify pieces of folklore that have become something else—antiquities, fixed, set, even fossilized.

All the material that might be included under the heading folklore shares the key characteristic of patterned repetition. The patterning may emerge in the language by which Homer describes a hero's preparation of a meal or his completion of it whenever such a scene appears in the *Odyssey*, that is, in the formulaic patterns of Homeric speech.[10] The patterning may appear in the repeated decorative motifs on a piece of Yoruba cloth or in the similar designs found on many such pieces of West African clothing.[11] Patterns are within single pieces of folklore or shared by pieces from the same culture. Certain patterns may recur cross-culturally or be traceable through lengthy periods of time.[12] Patterned repetition is thus of synchronic and diachronic interest. It is at the heart of all sorts of folklore and, on some level, an interest of all folklore scholarship, leading to questions such as the following: What is the configuration of the constituent units in a piece of folklore—a folktale or a piece of woven cloth? Can one establish a morphology that describes many tales of one culture or of several cultures? Can one trace the development of a traditional design over time such that the pattern evolves and changes? Do such patterns tell us something about the way traditional works are created, about the interaction between the creative individual and his or her culture? Are such patterns, in fact, templates in two senses, both guides to composition and reflections of the culture from which they come? Do the patterns of weaving or the narrative patterns of tales ultimately relate to larger symbolic systems, the worldview of a particular culture? Do cross-culturally shared patterns somehow reflect certain patterns of thought or concern common to all human beings?

My own interest in this study is in literature rather than in material culture, specifically in biblical narratives about unlikely successful heroes. With this particular interest as a focus and these wide-ranging questions as an entree, I set out to explore methodological approaches and interests of folklorists, taking note of what folklore scholarship has in common with traditional Bible scholarship and of new avenues that folklore offers. I will examine and assess what scholars of the Hebrew Scriptures have already done in folklore and suggest possible new directions. In subsequent chapters, I will apply folklore methodology to tales of underdogs and tricksters.

1. The Field of Folklore: A Review

Folklore scholarship may be examined in terms of three broad, overlapping categories: (1) *descriptive work*, which seeks to understand the form of a piece of folklore and to classify like pieces; (2) questions about *composition and transmission*, for example, how a piece is created, preserved, and handed down; (3) and questions about the *meaning, function, and context* of a piece.[1] How is it meaningful in the lives of individual authors and audiences? What relation does it have to the culture from which it stems or to the psyches of those who participate in it?

Description, Classification, Aesthetics

Contemporary folklorists share an emphasis on the "texture" of a piece of folk literature, by which is meant an examination of the very words, combinations of words, and style of the piece. In the concern with "texture" are echoes of the most traditional biblical concerns with philology, text-criticism, prosody, and, more recently, rhetorical criticism. An appreciation of this lowest level of structure, these primary building blocks, must precede the study of content. In a discussion of content and the combination of elements of content that make for narration—for "a specific text"[2]—the following major figures and methodologies emerge.

Classification and the Historic-Geographic School

The masterpieces of the Finnish, or Historic-Geographic, School are Antti Aarne and Stith Thompson's classificatory catalogues of folktale types and motifs.[3] By "motif" is meant the smallest reduceable piece of a tale—a character, an action, a magical instrument, a feature of setting—the building blocks, a combination of which make for the tale "type." The indices have a numbering system (e.g., nos. 460–499 are tale types about "supernatural tasks," 920–929 about "clever acts and words"; under letter B are "animal motifs," under K, "deceptions"). The names and details change with the cultural setting, but the type remains visible; the approach is taxonomic and cross-cultural. The Cinderella type (510), no matter where it occurs in the world, will always include an unlikely hero, unsupportive or hostile relatives, a magical helper, a recognition token, and so on—an essential combination of motifs that recurs in every example of the type.

Thompson and Aarne's interest in delineating types and motifs and in preparing a tale taxonomy was for a specific purpose—to trace the development of tales geographically and historically.[4] The members of the Finnish School believe that by collecting many examples of a type from all over the world and by plotting geographically the variations that occur in tellings of the tale they can trace its course of development. Matters of relative chronology are of interest also; a version that, for example, has a laser gun as the "magic instrument" is probably later than one in which it is a magic wand.

The Historic-Geographic School has been criticized by some contemporary folklorists for treating tales as self-generated literary phenomena, that is, for "taking the folk out of folklore," and for lack of attention to specific cultural milieux that give life and meaning to particular tellings of tales.[5] Unconvincing as the mappings of this school may be, Richard Dorson is correct in noting that the treasuries of tale types and motifs are enormously useful as indicators of the traditional.[6] If a biblical tale fits one of Thompson's types, the names, places, and settings being Israelite, we should be extremely cautious in drawing historical fact from the tale. The cross-cultural comparison made possible by the indices allows one to appreciate what is unique about the biblical tale and its culture and to recognize what is not unique. Overhistoricization remains an unhealthy scholarly preoccupation in biblical scholarship.[7] Folklorists too have long had an interest in distinguishing between history and folktale.[8] Bible scholars do not draw the distinction often enough, sometimes failing to take account of the kind of literature with which they are dealing and to note that certain motifs may be included in a tale because such tales traditionally just go a certain way.[9]

The Historic-Geographic interest in motifs and types is an implicit form of structuralism, making one think carefully about what goes into the content and form of a narrative, as shown by Dorothy Irvin's sensitive comparative study of several biblical and ancient Near Eastern non-Israelite tales.[10] Influenced by Stith Thompson's indices, by the work of Lord and Parry (discussed later), and continuing in the pioneering course charted by Gunkel's *Das Märchen im alten Testament*,[11] Irvin explores the tales' "plot-motifs" and "traditional episodes," categories akin to Propp's "functions" and Lord's and Parry's "themes." With the exception of Irvin's work, too little use has been made of the Thompson indices.[12] They will be helpful in an examination of underdogs and tricksters, though we must beware of the scattershot nature of Thompson's "structuralism" (if we can call it that), for the primary criterion in grouping tales is content at a quite specific level rather than overriding structure. Thus an "animal tale" (among types 1–299) may share an essential story line with a tale about humans (among "ordinary folktales," nos. 300–1199) but be types apart in Thompson's system. Similarly a motif that might be defined as "magic produces fertility" may be found in various guises throughout the Motif Index: T510, miraculous conception; T548, birth obtained through magic or prayer; D1347, magic object produces fecundity; D1927, fecundity magically induced. Another problem is the gray area between complex "motifs" and simple "types." That is, some of Thompson's "motifs" are sufficiently complex to qualify as "types," for example, T481.4, the Potiphar's wife plot.[13] These problems, significant though they are, do not disqualify the indices as useful tools in the examination of traditional tales, their content and form.

A. B. Lord and the Structure of Themes

Also significant in the exploration of motifs that combine to form types is the work of A. B. Lord, the great scholar of early and oral literature.[14] Lord's work will be discussed in detail under "transmission and composition" but is also an important guide to the traditional, even formulaic, combinations of content found in oral literature. Lord notes that oral narratives are composed of motifs joining together to form themes and themes linking together in thematic chains. Lord's definition of motif is the same as Thompson's. The theme of the hero's return may be composed of the presence of the faithful servant, the recognition token, the disguise of the hero, the hostility of rivals, and so on. The theme of return may follow a battle theme, itself composed of traditional motifs. Such is the stuff of traditional composition. As in the tale-teller's choice of language, the choice and combination of content is a variation on a flexible but expected set of possibilities; there are ways to compose certain sorts of tales in particular cultures—motifs, clusters of motifs, and patterns of themes expected by audiences and ready for authors who compose extemporaneously in a process of oral composition. The structures of content uncovered by Lord reflect compositional techniques, the way a piece of traditional literature comes to be the way it is. His sensitive approach to the patterning of stories, the compositional stuff of narrative, however, provides another valuable model in describing the literary forms of the Bible, one applicable to the study of a narrative of Genesis or the form of a prophetic oracle. In the latter case the themes are the "forms" of form-criticism, the chains of forms comprising the oracle as a whole.[15] Lord, like Thompson, works cross-culturally. His comparison of Serbo-Croatian and Homeric epic, undertaken to prove the oral composition of the Greek material, also shows more broadly how narrative works and how certain patterns of motifs or themes are shared across times and cultures. His work, like that of Thompson, encourages us more often to set biblical narrative in the context of the tales of other cultures, not merely in the context of the literature of its closest ancient Near Eastern neighbors. Further contribution to this cross-cultural approach is made by David Bynum.[16] By tracking various motif combinations, Bynum shows the remarkable stability of certain patterns of human narrative discourse and heightens our appreciation of them. For Bynum, the initiation tale of an African epic hero sheds light on the form, message, and meaning of the Samson tale, in places even illuminating seemingly obscure points in this or that narrative with the deceptively simple explanation that tales of a certain kind work this way. He describes the contents of tales in terms of "generic" and "nominal" motifs, the generic motif being the universal, for example, the trickster, the nominal being the specification of that motif in a specific tale, for example, the Abram of Genesis 12.[17] There are in fact degrees of specificity between the generic and the nominal, graduated layers of reference that figure in the analysis in later chapters. Bynum's treatment of motif moves in this direction.

Lord's findings have been employed by Bible scholars in matters of composition, but his and Bynum's studies have further relevance, leading one to view the building blocks of traditional narrative as dynamic, the tales themselves as manifestations of a quintessentially human activity, story telling.

Lord's work shares with more overtly structuralist approaches an interest in the arrangement of and relation between the building blocks of a piece of literature. Such approaches to traditional literature include the Russian formalism of Vladimir Propp, several related treatments of genres of folklore, and the structuralism of the French anthropologist Claude Lévi-Strauss.[18]

Propp's "Formalism"

Analyzing the content and structure of one hundred Russian tales, numbers 50–151 of the Afanas'ev collection, Propp finds a single morphology that describes all of them. Propp concerns himself not with this or that particular rendition of content— not with the "etic" level of content as Dundes calls it, after Kenneth Pike[19]—but with the functions of the tales' characters in the action structure of the narrative. A function such as "hero acquires the use of a magical agent" (function XIV)[20] may be filled in various ways. Recall Bynum's distinction between generic and nominal motifs. The hero may be a soldier or a prince, the agent, a magical sword or a flying horse, but the functions are "stable, constant elements of limited number"; their "sequence," moreover, is always identical.[21] In Dundes's and Pike's terms of "etic" and "emic," the pattern of "moti-femes" is a constant that may be filled in by various "etic" motifs in each particular rendering of the morphology.[22] Propp's work, concerned with narrative components and combinations, is an important guide to uncovering the working parts of traditional narrative. As is the case for Thompson's work, the very delineation of these parts is a useful aesthetic exercise and a first step to further work, but as Dundes has noted, Propp's *Morphology* falls short of asking any of the "how" and "for what purpose" questions. Where do such patterns come from? Why do they seem to be universal?[23]

The newly translated collection of Propp's work indicates in Propp's defense that he was indeed concerned with many of these questions, viewing the *Morphology* as a preliminary descriptive exercise that must precede "historical inquiry."[24] On the other hand, his mode of description might be criticized for being too synchronic and monochromatic in its capacity to describe elements of content.[25] Even though Propp, like Bynum, Dundes, and Jason, is sensitive to the "transformations" undergone by tales in the context of a particular cultural setting,[26] his insistence on the invariability of the sequence of functions, his overemphasis on actions rather than actors, and his conclusion that there is only one type of Russian "wondertale" have all been questioned in recent scholarship.[27] Propp provides a useful model for tracing the narrative forms of the Old Testament, indeed, a tool of form-criticism, but one must be wary, as one should be with all form-criticism, of forcing biblical texts into a pattern that Propp deduced from one hundred Russian folktales of a certain type. It is for this reason that attempts like that of J. M. Sasson to set Ruth on the Proppian grid are not satisfying.[28] Such treatments of biblical narrative risk having a wooden or mechanistic quality. More flexible and profound are investigations like those of Robert Culley, which though strongly influenced by Propp do not attempt to squeeze biblical tales into Propp's schema. Allowing biblical texts their own patterning, Culley examines their "action sequences," attempting to understand better the workings of individual biblical narratives.[29] It is important to remember that the study of variants is important to Propp and to folklorists. Too often Bible scholars set Propp's scheme against one Old Testament tale whereas it might be more useful to collect like biblical material, employing Propp's work as a model and guide in establishing biblical morphologies. Dan Ben-Amos's morphological treatment of rabbinic tales and Alan Dundes's examination of North American Indian tales deserve emulation.[30]

Related Classificatory Work

Several other scholars should be mentioned in connection with Propp since they, like Propp, sought to uncover key underlying traits shared by certain varieties of folk literature. André Jolles's description of the genres of folklore[31] have influenced Claus Westermann's treatment of the patriarchal narratives as family saga,[32] and Carl Wilhelm von Sydow's complex classificatory system for folk narrative[33] figures in Albert de Pury's study of the Jacob narrative.[34] Of enduring influence in folklore studies is Max Lüthi's study of *Märchen*,[35] the sort of tales in the Thompson Type-Index 300–749 (tales of magic). Monumental and important as the works of von Sydow and Jolles are, they have become genre traps for scholars of the Old Testament. If a biblical narrative displays many of the traits of a European folktale designated *"Märchen"* by Jolles and other scholars of European literature, it does not necessarily follow that it is or "originally" was like Jolles's *Märchen* in all respects—completely fictional, universal, nonspecific in historical date and setting, and so on.[36] It is equally misleading to suggest that if a biblical tale deals with specific ancestor heroes in a historical setting it is saga on the Icelandic model.[37] Such genre-superimposing, genre-matching approaches add little to our understanding of the tale, its form, function, or meaning in Israelite culture. Max Lüthi makes it quite clear that he deals with a specifically European phenomenon. The applicability of his work to a wider range of materials remains to be seen.[38] Better to let the tales speak for themselves. In a study of the content and form of Israelite narrative certain morphologically based Israelite genres may emerge, but we do well to remember that actual "ethnic genres" may well clash with external, "analytical categories of classification."[39] More helpful than classifications such as *Märchen* or *Sage* may be morphological definitions of genre based on overall structure of content[40] not on this or that feature of content or setting.[41]

In a related category are the cross-cultural studies of J. G. von Hahn, Otto Rank, and Lord Raglan, which point to a recurring pattern of elements associated with the "hero."[42] Alan Dundes's provocative study of "hero patterns" in the Jesus traditions[43] and Ronald Hendel's recent work on the Jacob narrative[44] suggest that the "hero pattern" may provide interesting avenues of exploration in our study of underdogs and tricksters.

Particularly influential among works seeking to uncover *topoi* and genres in folklore has been Axel Olrik's "Epic Laws of Folk Narrative," in which Olrik points to traits he believes to be shared by all *Sage*.[45] Included among these characteristics are single-strandedness of plot, repetitions in threes, and a slow easing in and easing out of the story. Olrik's laws of *Sage* influenced Hermann Gunkel and still influence many modern scholars' assessment of the nature of ancient Hebrew narrative. In applying Olrik's work to Old Testament narrative, some things should be kept in mind. By *Sage*, Olrik did not refer to epic or myth or folktale or Icelandic saga, but rather to these genres and to all other traditional narrative forms, including folksong and ballad. This realization should make one cautious about loose uses of the word *saga* or *Sage* in Bible studies. In referring to Olrik we may also wish to distance ourselves from some of his assumptions. Olrik's study, like that of Thompson, worries little about composers, creators, and audiences, assuming that literary traditions are forces in and of themselves. Do Bible scholars who find Olrik helpful wish to share in these assumptions about the "superorganic forces" behind traditional literature? Apparent adherence to Olrik's laws by a narrative, moreover, does not necessarily mean it was orally composed (contra Gunkel)[46] or that it is earlier in date than works that do not exhibit these laws (contra Van Seters).[47]

Lévi-Strauss and Deep Structures

The other major structuralist approach popular in folklore is, of course, that of the towering French anthropologist Claude Lévi-Strauss. In contrast to Propp, who deals with the pattern of events—the diachronic pattern of folktales—Lévi-Strauss is interested in a synchronic "deep structure" in the tale.[48] Like other structuralists, Lévi-Strauss divides the narrative into components or constituent units, but he goes beyond the plot-line order of units, detaching them from their place in this diachronic pattern and exploring the synchronic relationships between them. Here we find an assumption by Lévi-Strauss that humans perceive the world in contrasting pairs or dichotomies—life versus death, divine versus human, nature versus culture—and that these contrasts are symbolizations and affirmations of the contrary conditions of our existence and the confusions in our psyches. We long for immortality and yet die; as the rabbis say, we speak like the angels and yet defecate and die like animals. We are of twos. To cope with these irresolvables, the symbol systems reflected in various aspects of our culture, rituals and other lore, include third items that share traits of both sides of the dichotomy, thereby transforming the conflicting dyad into a harmonious triad—imbalance becomes balance. The conflict is not erased but is made part of a larger system that suggests wholeness. Thus a holy man, able to perform miracles and connect to the realm of the divine, is nevertheless a human who eats and lives on earth. Lévi-Strauss suggests that one can uncover whole series or "bundles" of contrasting and mediated pairs in the deep structures of myths such as the tale of Oedipus in its various versions or the Coyote trickster tales of the Jicarilla Apache. One might question whether our thinking is so dichotomous—if so, is this a Western phenomenon?[49] As in all structuralist approaches, is one in danger of superimposing idiosyncratic patterns on literature, so that one ends up with a new phenomenon: a reflection of the complex and fascinating mind of Lévi-Strauss and not of the Apache worldview?[50] Were the ancient Greeks really worried about the question of the autochthonous origins of humankind[51] or the Israelites about the incest of the first couple who are of the same flesh and become one flesh, as Edmond Leach concludes in his well-known and controversial structuralist study?[52] Is it valid to consider all the versions of a tale reflections of the same myth? Is not each version of the Oedipus story a unique creation, reflecting its own author and audience, as well as a thread in a larger web of relationships?

In spite of the validity of some of these criticisms, the work of Robert Oden, Robert Polzin, and others shows that, sensitively applied, Lévi-Strauss's structuralism has much to teach us about the dynamics of biblical narrative, about the symbol structures of Israelite literature and cult, and about the marginality, the in-betweenness, characterizing the biblical heroes of this study.[53] In fact, the culture-specific, ethnographic, and anthropological orientation of Lévi-Strauss's structuralism should not be forgotten. His work is equally relevant to our discussion of meanings, culture, and folklore in context. Important also is his emphasis on variants, what Leach refers to as an emphasis on redundancy; important narrative themes recur in cultures, with fascinating nuances.[54] The variants, treated synchronically as different faces of the same tale, may provide a better understanding each of the other and an understanding of the larger worldview of the culture from which they come.

Conclusions on "The Descriptive"

These then are some of the questions folklorists pose and the methodologies they employ in describing and dissecting an item of folklore. Some of the approaches discussed have much in common with traditional Bible scholarship; others already have been employed in Bible studies with varying degrees of success; and others deserve new attention or different emphasis among students of the Bible.

All folkloristic approaches discussed have a certain structuralist interest, be it the taxonomic work of the Finnish School, with its cataloguing of motifs and motif combinations that are types, the function-outline of Propp, the motifs and themes of Lord and Bynum, or the deep structures of Lévi-Strauss. Though Propp has been influential and instructive in sensitive hands, there is danger in woodenly fitting biblical tales onto his grid. Lévi-Strauss's approach has led to some fascinating if controversial suggestions, but applications have not taken seriously enough his emphasis on the importance of versions and variants, working with only one tale at a time. Thompson's indices and the approaches of Lord and Bynum have not been employed sufficiently to place Old Testament literature in the context of comparative folk literature or to help in understanding the sort of narrative literature with which we are dealing. Finally, one must remember that certain characteristics that identify biblical narrative as traditional do not necessarily indicate oral traditional composition.

Composition and Transmission

How does any particular piece of folk literature come to be as it is? How has it been preserved? These are questions of composition and transmission. Students of biblical poetry have in the past been most attuned to these issues, assuming that there is some system, metrical or syllabic, leading to the selection of certain words and to the combination of words in a piece.

Questions of composition and transmission in the context of Bible studies evoke various methodologies: source criticism, which suggests that one can ascertain the sources or documents out of which were woven portions of the Bible; redaction criticism, by which one attempts to track the formation of this or that piece of the tradition, a single pericope or a whole book; tradition-history, which traces recurring themes to uncover stages in the tradition, trajectories of tradition; and composition criticism, in which one pays special attention to the final preservers or composers of a piece. Articles such as "The Survival of Indo-European Mythology in Germanic Legendry" appearing in the *Journal of American Folklore* suggest that the "what-came-from-where-when-and-how" approaches to tradition are found also in contemporary folklore scholarship.[55] The work of the Finnish School, which attempts to trace the development and diffusion of tale types, and the studies of scholars such as Jan Vansina and Walter Anderson, who discuss rules under which oral traditions develop and change, are, in some senses, the folklorist's answer to the Bible scholar's redaction and tradition-history criticism.[56]

Yet in some respects biblical and folklorist versions of redaction criticism and tradition-history share the same weaknesses. Too often Old Testament scholars imagine the process of composition and transmission to involve individuals in scriptoria, redactors, editors, and compilers rather that composers practicing their art in accordance with a set of cultural expectations for those who share in that culture.[57] At the same time, though intensely interested in transmission history, Thompson does not ask about composers and cultural contexts but implies that the tale has a life of its own. Similarly, Propp never explores how his stable set of functions contributes to the composition and handing down of tales, though he is not unaware of the importance of these questions.[58] The scriptorium should not be abandoned in dealing with traditional-style biblical literature, only to adopt a superorganic force. Similarly, the Bible scholar's concern with Ur-forms, first, original versions of pieces of literature, find a parallel in the historical-geographic scholar's search for the place where a tale type originates, a search implying that one can ascertain the earliest form of a tale. Contemporary folklorists such as Dan Ben-Amos suggest, to the contrary, that multiplicity is at the heart of all folklore; tales always exist in multiplicity. These folklorists' interest is in understanding this or that version in context, not in hunting for Ur-forms, a fresh approach to emulate in exploring the traditional-style narratives of Scripture.[59]

The work of students of early and oral literature—Parry, Lord, Bynum—and of modern folklorists such as Del Hymes, Dan Ben-Amos, Kenneth Goldstein, and Alan Dundes richly explores questions about composition and multiplicity, about the creative individual and cultural forces that shape a piece, allowing it to be transmitted and in the process to change and not change, that is, to be remarkably stable in some respects and always fresh, new, and altered at the same time.

The studies of Lord and Parry, suggesting and testing criteria for proving that the *Iliad* and the *Odyssey* were orally composed, have already been mined by Bible scholars. David Gunn's careful analysis of patterns of content and language in Judges and Samuel points to the strongly traditional quality of portions of these books, raising the possibility of roots in oral story-telling traditions.[60] There has been a less careful tendency in biblical studies, however, to assert that this or that piece is "oral literature" without real attention to the implications, linguistic and contextual, of that description; namely, that a piece has been composed extemporaneously by a skilled professional learned in the manipulation of formulaic patterns of speech and content that he or she freshly combines to form traditional tales.[61] Dennis MacDonald's recent work on the apocryphal tales of Paul is to be commended for its attention to the traditional patterns of content found in the tales. This study, like Boling's commentary on Judges, is attuned to differences between traditional and nontraditional literature.[62] The presence of traditional patterning, however, does not allow the scholar to leap to the conclusion that the material originally was orally composed by traveling tale-tellers—in this way to reconstruct a sociology behind the tales. More cautious are the studies of William Whallon, Robert Culley, John Kselman, William J. Urbrock, and others who explore the possibility that Old Testament poetry exhibits oral style (Culley, Urbrock, Whallon) or that certain prose pieces may have origins in oral poetry and exhibit hints of that past (Kselman).[63] These are studies of compositional significance. Culley's work and that of others[64] makes varying suggestions for the ways in which the pairs of Hebrew poetry, long cited as central to the semiotics of ancient Hebrew poetry,[65] may be involved in more complex formula patterns. Increasingly, however, as a fine collection of essays in *Semeia* indicates, scholars are beginning to move beyond considerations of the formula and proofs for oral composition or origins.[66] The work on this lowest level may have taught us as much as it can. One will never be able to assert absolutely that any piece of Old Testament literature was orally composed.[67] The sample available in the Old Testament to test for formulaic patterns is simply too small, such proofs being based on recurrence. One cannot recover oral poetry from prose; nor, perhaps, should one. The line between prose and poetry in traditional-style literature, in any event, is a less clear one than even Culley implies.[68]

The search for formulas and the hypotheses about oral composition, however, have been crucial first steps in thinking afresh about the nature of biblical literary tradition, providing evidence on the level of texture that biblical literature is traditional in style, if not necessarily orally composed, and creating a host of important new challenges to Old Testament scholarship. Emphasizing the relationship between formulaic language and content, for example, Susan Wittig asks how formulas are generated, how traditional-style narratives function in a culture.[69] A scholar such as Del Hymes explores further the boundary where linguistics meets sociology. How is the very pattern of speech found in a piece of folk literature a reflection of culture?[70]

The realization that much of biblical literature in form and content is traditional literature, if not necessarily or provably orally composed literature, makes one think twice, moreover, about "borrowing" or "copying with nuances" as an explanation for why a biblical narrative looks like those of non-Israelite ancient Near Eastern literatures or why Genesis 12 looks so much like Genesis 20 or Genesis 26. Works similar in content and structure may better be viewed as an individual author's creative expression of a pattern shared with others in a culture, Israelite, ancient Near Eastern or Mediterranean.[71]

The folklorist's interest in a context of performance and the form-critic's emphasis on *Sitz im Leben*, or life-setting, are important methodological links between folklore and Bible studies. The notion of *Sitz* is usually conceived more narrowly, however, than folklorists' notion of context. To suggest that the setting of a biblical narrative poem might be "the cult" says a great deal less about modes of composition and transmission than to note that tellers of tales adapt their telling to audiences[72] or to suggest that tales that neatly fit the types of Thompson's Index have been transmitted by professionals skilled at telling tales "the right way," not by some more arbitrary process.[73] Though I do not suggest that all or most of the traditional literature of the Bible was performed, emphases implicit in the performance image on communication, cultural setting, creators of literature, and receivers of the literature do challenge us to think again about "life-settings" of biblical literature and especially about the meaning of a "Yahwist" or an "Elohist," an epic source or a court writer, those to whom this or that traditional-style piece is assigned.[74]

In discussing composition and transmission, finally, we do well to avoid falling into old generalizations of folklorists that are now out of date in that field, for example, that traditional-style lore comes from rural, peasant contexts,[75] that the folklore is necessarily what is oldest in the tradition, or that all true folk tradition is orally transmitted.[76]

Some Conclusions

One should not replace source and redaction theories with the folklorists' superorganic force. For modern folklorists, performance is the thing; literature is understood as process, as communication within a cultural context allowing for the importance of creative composers and attentive, empathetic audiences.

One cannot prove that biblical literature is oral literature, but studies exploring the Bible and oral literature have had an enlightening, aesthetically sensitizing mission, confirming that much of biblical literature even in its current form shares much in style of language and form of content with oral literature. Biblical literature is traditional literature if "traditional" is defined as in the Introduction. We are therefore encouraged to consider the implications of literature as communication in a cultural context, to take full account of the expectations of authors and audiences in a sensitive new sort of biblical composition and form-criticism. Current folklore scholarship leads me away from redaction and tradition history, though such interests are found in the field of folklore itself. Folklore, however, reinforces old-fashioned Bible-scholar interests in sociological and historical setting, for in contrast to some modern literary critics, folklorists are not content to consider texts as texts in and of themselves but view them as integral parts of particular value systems grounded in time and place.

Folklore in Context: Meaning, Personal and Communal

The fields of anthropology, sociology, and psychology contribute to the interdiscipline that is folklore. Folklorists enter these fields with their own special bent and interests in order to understand the place of pieces of folklore in contemporary cultural settings, in lengthy cultural traditions, or in the lives of individuals. How is a piece of folklore an expression of human conditions, both psychological and cultural?

Like students of classical Greek epic, would-be folklorists of the Bible face limitations. Languages dealt with are no longer spoken or written in their ancient forms; one cannot question informants or assess cultural settings at first hand. In short, the firsthand material that is at the heart of the analysis of the anthropologist, sociologist, or psychologist is lacking; yet a cautious application of these disciplines can lead to exciting speculations worth making.

In anthropology and sociology, the work of Bible scholars is sophisticated and dynamic and by now well recognized in the field. Robert R. Wilson's pioneering study of prophecy and his earlier work on the genealogy richly indicate that the modes of religious expression found in live cultures can help us to understand those of ancient Israel.[77]

Many of the applications of anthropology to study of the Bible have to do with religious institutions, prophecy or regulations governing purity, and there is still more to add to Mary Douglas's classic study of the Kashrut laws and other ways in which ancient Israelites (or the composers of these laws) symbolically compartmentalized aspects of their life experience in the ongoing effort to keep chaos at bay. There are other pieces of the symbol system worth exploring, laws pertaining to reproduction and menstruation being among them. Lévi-Strauss's techniques might also be fruitfully applied to the ritual symbolism of the Hebrew Scriptures. In all these cases one must remember that the Bible contains not ritual reports of trained observers but literature presenting ritual and ritual law.

However, for the purposes of our study of hero tales, another problem arises. Are anthropological interests and approaches helpful in exploring the narrative literature of the Hebrew Scriptures, not rituals or institutions but tales?

Anthropologists, of course, must work with the sacred tales of the cultures they study. Though anthropologists of previous generations were functionalist in their study of myths, assuming in Radcliffe-Brown's famous axiom that religion parallels social structure,[78] modern scholars such as Clifford Geertz have a more dynamic approach attuned to the working of symbols in various genres, writing of these symbols' capacity not only to reflect but also to affect cultures.[79] Like modern folklorists, who tend to question Western scholars' sometimes superficial and culturally superimposed distinctions between various folk genres,[80] increasingly, anthropologists have become interested in the cultural boundary where sacred tales meet literature, rituals meet drama, and all converge on the plane of poetics and metaphor.[81] Thus ritual patterns like the rite of passage may well have relevance for the Joseph *Bildungsroman*.

Contemporary anthropologists, like folklorists, moreover, warn against viewing cultures as neat monoliths mapped out consistently in myth and ritual. Again the particular performer and the variegations of individual performances are important; there is no ideal, unsullied "Ur-form" of a particular myth, for example, an important reminder for practitioners of form-criticism as well.[82] Diversity in the telling of this or that sort of tale is an important indicator of diversities, complexities, even tensions in a culture, for no culture is static, no representation of it in literary or dramatic lore normative in some absolute or simple sense.

Anthropologists have not always shown themselves especially sensitive to or interested in texts as literature. For the folklorist, the native informant who presents and preserves a tale is a creative artist, composer, or performer. The folklorist's anthropology not only treats the tale as a dynamic symbolization of worldview and ethos in Geertz's terms (i.e., of the metaphysic, the view of the very structure of the cosmos, and the values, the way of life, tone, style of living) but also as an example of traditional literature whose particular style, narrative structure, and context of presentation matter. Attention to the creative form of the tale, in fact, leads to a greater understanding of the culture from which its creator comes and of the worldview it expresses. It is this sort of literarily sensitive cultural anthropology one brings to the tales of Old Testament heroes.

Folklorist-sociologists specialize in describing and assessing the social setting of a folklore performance or process. What is the performer's role within and relationship to the group? What are the social influences on his or her performance? Like other sociologists, folklorists attempt to describe what makes for a community and a social milieu. The folklorists, however, have a more specific interest in social influences on performers and folklore and, in turn, the effect that the lore, performer, and specific performances have on a social world. Sociologically oriented folklorists are interested in matters of class and gender and in demography, employing questionnaires, statistical surveys, and informants to ascertain the makeup of the community from whom the lore comes.[83]

Although, once again, working with a live culture differs from working with a dead one, and although sociological methodologies need to be applied with caution, certain aspects and varieties of sociological theory have been applied to the Hebrew Scriptures with interesting results. Continuing and expanding upon the seminal work of George Mendenhall, Norman Gottwald challenges old and loose notions of "tribe" and "seminomadic" as sociological categories, emphasizing rural versus urban and rich versus poor conflicts as crucial in an understanding of the conquest period.[84] Gottwald creatively employs biblical texts and archaeological and other extrabiblical material to ask sociological questions of ancient cultures and communities.

As in the case of anthropology, folklorists approach sociology with special literary interests that make their version of the field appropriate for study of the traditional literature of the Bible. Their contextual approach deals with authors and audiences in social settings. Roger D. Abrahams writes about "Personal Power and Social Restraint in the Definition of Folklore,"[85] and Richard Bauman of "Differential Identity and the Social Base of Folklore."[86] Even though the preparers of our material cannot be questioned at first hand, the literature itself can serve as an informant if one asks the right questions. Does the material betray certain attitudes to authority? to gender? to people of a certain age? What hierarchies or pecking orders emerge in the literature? Who is "us" and who "them"? Like anthropological theory, sociological questions are often applied to institutions, movements, and historical and prophetic texts. They are also relevant to the traditional-style narratives of this study, as the work of folklorists demonstrates.

Of particular importance in asking questions about authority and gender is the field of women's studies, which has added important dimensions to folkloristics, as it has to so many areas of the humanities and social sciences. Scholars of women's studies and folklore explore images of women in folk materials, literary and nonliterary, searching for the possible symbolic resonances behind recurring motifs.[87] They seek to understand roles of and attitudes toward women in particular cultures by studying their characterizations in folktale, ballad, or folk art[88] and their social standing as narrators of tales, practioners of forms of folk wisdom, or performers of folk art.[89] What sort of narratives do women tell in particular cultures and with what significance?[90] Does women's lore provide alternative social models to those provided by men's lore in the culture?[91] A fascinating paper explores how the Grimm brothers altered collected material before publication to "render [portraits of mother figures] less powerful, more stereotypical and better conforming to Victorian ideals."[92] Models provided by women's studies and folklore give added dimension to our study of the matriarchs and Esther.

Whereas anthropological and sociological treatments of folklore deal with the meanings and messages of particular cultures and communities, psychoanalytical approaches are reminders that pieces of folklore express aspects of the humanness that all people share, the emotional concerns and stages that define each of us. One of the major proponents of psychoanalytical approaches to folklore is Alan Dundes, whose work is Freudian in bent—Oedipal nuances, fear of one's sexuality, fear of castration emerge for him in the symbolic patterns of folk literature.[93] He and other Freudians have been criticized for superimposing sexual connotations whenever possible: phallic beanstocks or womblike ovens.[94] Yet Freudian theories about the role of family relationships in human development may provide great insight into the recurring patterns of family interaction found in Genesis. Why do certain types of family stories recur in Scripture and in a larger corpus of world cultures? Is a set of symbolic values at work in such narratives that transcends any particular culture? Rank's Freudian analysis of hero narratives, relevant to the study of underdogs and tricksters, attempts to provide answers to some of these wide-ranging questions,[95] as do the Jungian-influenced studies of Joseph Campbell and Erich Neumann, which suggest that the stages of human development are reflected in shared symbols or archetypes visible in the artifacts of all cultures throughout all human history.[96] For a scholar such as Neumann, the human psyche is a microcosm of the history of individual cultures and the larger patterns of human social history, all of which ideally undergo the transformation from undifferentiation to differentiation, from unconsciousness to consciousness. Although such notions of human development, individual and cultural, may be suspect, the study of traditional narratives may nevertheless be enriched by Jungian emphases on transformation and stages and attention to recurring patterns in the products of human creativity.

Conclusions on "Folklore in Context"

The study of "folklore in context" finds parallels in Old Testament scholars' applications of sociology, anthropology, and women's studies to the study of Scripture. Folklore scholarship challenges the student of Scripture, however, to employ these theoretical approaches to understand not only Israelite institutions, social movements, and cultic practices but also narrative traditions. Patterns that characterize ritual "rites of passage," for example, may well be applicable to tales about the maturation of the hero. Patterns of thought found in aspects of social structure and ritual may be equally apparent in literature—all of which may reflect certain essential and shared aspects of human consciousness.

To the Texts

The theoretical approaches and interests of folklore lead finally to the texts. As in the work of folklorists such as Alan Dundes and Richard Dorson, the methodology in this study will be eclectic. Certain broad threads that have been emphasized in this chapter and important to all folklorists run throughout: the concern with patterning, the interest in cross-cultural comparison, concern with performance and author-audience issues, and interest in "context" and setting as understood by the interdiscipline folklore.

2. The Three Wife-Sister Tales of Genesis

The three tales about the patriarch who tells the foreigners that his wife is his sister are all about heroes whose less than propitious early circumstances turn to success and elevation; marginality and insecurity are replaced by wealth and higher, more secure status. Genesis 12:10–20, 20:1–18, and 26:1–17, of course, share each other's content and plot more closely. Not only are they all underdog tales, but at first reading they seem to be versions of the same underdog story: variants, the very stuff that folklore is made of and the perfect starting point for our study.

The wife-as-sister tales have been of lively interest to a variety of scholars. Traditional commentaries often treat them as case studies in source criticism, assigning 12:10–20 and 26:1–17 to the Yahwist and 20:1–18, with its dreams and prevalent "Elohim" names for God, to the Elohist.[1] Klaus Koch's *Growth of the Biblical Tradition* exemplifies a Bible scholar's source-critical, form-critical, redaction-critical, and tradition-critical treatment of such variants and many of the potential weaknesses of such approaches to traditional-style literature. Koch believes that all three tales stem from an Ur-version and sets out to reconstruct a common original from the "oldest-seeming" elements in each extant version.[2] Folklorists would suggest that such searches for originals are fruitless—better to assess each version as performance, regarding all multiforms in the tradition as equally valid performances. Like Claus Westermann, Koch accepts the saga model for the tales, calling them ethnological sagas.[3] A folklorist would doubt the relevance to Israelite narrative of Jolles's views of an Icelandic genre, as has

John Van Seters.[4] Koch's notion of orally transmitted literature
is unsophisticated; he suggests, for instance, that brevity is a
criterion of oral transmission, whereas orally transmitted works
like the epics of the Milman Parry collection may be quite
lengthy. Koch makes no reference to genuine criteria of oral
composition. Finally, Koch's description of life-setting is based
in part on a peculiar equation between the patriarchs' wives
and "bedouin" spouses.[5]

Koch's work has a precursor in that of the great Hermann
Gunkel. From Gunkel come the descriptive categories ethnographic and ethnological saga.[6] In Gunkel one finds the same
emphasis on brevity as a sign of oral composition.[7] Yet in spite
of these misdirections, in spite of his romantic view of the folk
and of the early "poetic" composers of Scripture, in spite of an
evolutionary bent that assumes that oral traditions are always
earlier than written ones, and in spite of his continued faith in
a documentary hypothesis greatly weakened by his own rejection of J and E as genuine authors,[8] Gunkel had enormous
literary sensitivity. His comparison between stark and primitive
tales and baroque ones is excellent; his emphasis on the importance of variants and on legends as reflections of worldview
is worthy of a contemporary folklorist, as is his realization, in
contrast to Koch, that one can never reconstruct a first version
of a tale.[9] For reasons of style and content, Gunkel finds the
wife-sister tale in Genesis 12 to be earliest and in this is followed recently by John Van Seters.[10] Gunkel and Van Seters
concentrate on the relationship among the three accounts, their
comparability, as does Samuel Sandmel, who suggests that the
tales exemplify inner-biblical *aggadah*.[11] One version "corrects"
and explains another. The impression of an ethically ambiguous
Abram conveyed by chapter 12, for example, is "neutralized"
by the account in chapter 20, which has Abraham declare that
indeed Sarah is his sister, his half-sister. One might question
not only whether the tale traditions interact in this way but
also whether the phenomenon described by Sandmel is aggadic
midrash at all. Sandmel, like Gunkel and Van Seters, does sen-

sitize us, however, to differences in the accounts that raise questions about the tellers of the tales and their audiences.

Other treatments of the wife-sister narratives are more synchronic, exploring each as a version of one tale in its varieties. Influenced by the structural anthropology of Claude Lévi-Strauss, who regards all the versions of a myth ultimately as a single myth, Robert Polzin finds recurring messages in the three versions concerning adultery, wealth, progeny, and God's blessing.[12] Polzin's work suggests a further question: Why is this basic story so popular? Does it reveal something essential about an Israelite self-image or worldview?

Influenced by the work of Robert Alter,[13] James G. Williams suggests that Genesis 12, 20, and 26 exemplify variations on a formulaic convention or type-scene, "the wife/sister scene." Williams explores the way in which each author uniquely employs a basic pattern well recognized in its essentials by an audience. Though Williams's approach pays full respect to what is special about each account, to its author's intentions and the expectations of its audience, implicit in it is the assertion that there exists a stylized or ideal version of the tale pattern, shared by a particular group. Such an assertion is possible when abstracting a conventional pattern from scores of Western movies, the example Williams employs (after Alter) to explain his understanding of a typological or stock narrative pattern.[14] Is the typological so obvious, however, when one has only three versions of the pattern? Surely additional controls are needed. Nevertheless the suggestion that each version is a variant of a particular narrative pattern is an important one, offered also by Robert Culley.[15] Culley's interest and approach move close to those of the present study. Culley outlines the patterns of content found in each account of the wife-sister tale, contrasting and comparing them. He provides a review of scholarship on oral narrative and asks whether the wife-sister tales are oral variants, written ones, or something between the two. His review of folklore scholarship leads him wisely to warn against easy solutions to problems of relative chronology.

Culley's approach, which, like that of Williams, pays full attention to each telling of the tale as an individual composition, begins to suggest new questions about the wife-sister tales and other clusters of biblical narrative that exhibit recognizably similar patterns of content. Their work does not presuppose the existence of neatly definable strands in Genesis, nor is it concerned with the existence of an Ur-version, contra Koch, or with identifying the earliest extant version, contra Gunkel and Van Seters. Culley and Williams think in terms of authors and audiences to whom and for whom each telling of the tale would have been relevant and meaningful. It is possible to go further and deeper than these scholars, however, asking of the tales the full range of folklorists' questions outlined in chapter 1, cross-cultural comparison between the biblical tales and other comparable works being especially helpful.

In this study, framed by the concerns of folklorists, as in those of Culley, Williams, and Van Seters, a good place to begin analysis is with a close examination of the narrative structure of the tales. The pattern outlined by each of these scholars has a certain validity and usefulness, yet each emphasizes different pieces of content or refers to the elements by more or less specific terms. Each outline leads to different thrusts, themes, and questions of the text. Each, though interesting, is somehow incomplete or imprecise. For example, Van Seters's outline of Genesis 12—(*a*) situation of need, problem, or crisis, (*b*) plan to deal with the problem (wise or foolish), (*c*) the execution of the plan with some complication, (*d*) an unexpected outside intervention, (*e*) fortunate or unfortunate consequences—leads him quickly and matter-of-factly to suggest that Genesis 12 is an Israelite version of a common variety of story exemplified by the Arab tale collected and translated in Schmidt and Kahle's *Volkserzählungen aus Palästina*, "Die verkleidete Frau."[16] When one reads the Arab tale, a story of a cuckolded husband, one wonders, however, where the similarities between this tale and Genesis 12 lie. They share elements on a "generic" level of content, but they do not share elements at a more specific level. Should not an examination of the wife-sister tales analyze the narratives on various "planes of expression and content," to borrow a phrase from Robert Polzin?[17]

A. Julien Greimas and others in his scholarly tradition deal with the complex multilayered quality of narrative form and content by combining Proppian sequential analysis with synchronic Lévi-Straussian examination of a tale's "deep structure."[18] Our interest here is not in "deep structure" but in the multiplicity of layers contained in the narrative's sequential pattern, in the story itself as presented. Toward this end, the analysis that follows provides an overlay map. Moving slowly from a description of each text's language to an initial, basic description of its content, and then to increasingly specific and detailed levels of description, we seek to understand what constitutes each version of this tale, its structure and content, how or if it can be compared to works produced in other cultures, and how its themes might have appealed to a certain kind of author and audience.

Wording and Texture

A first responsibility is to ask, where necessary, philological and text-critical questions of the text in order to be comfortable with the language of the passage before proceeding to stylistic analysis. The analysis of style explores how the author employs language, be it repetitious or not, simple and stark or baroque, and so on. A careful examination of the language of the work necessarily leads to an exploration of content and the way that content is structured. Just as individual words are chosen and combined to form meaningful phrases, so pieces of content join to form structures. We move from wording and texture to text or narration, in Jason's terms. But how does one define these pieces or elements of content?

In fact, the pieces may be described on various levels or planes, which move from the general to the specific, each level of description providing new insight into the workings of the narrative, into its relationship to other literary works, biblical and nonbiblical, and into its various meanings, implicit and explicit.

Narration

Generic Elements

The major steps of the narrative are described in lowest-common-denominator terms such as *problem* or *outcome*. The steps are narrative blanks that may be filled in numerous ways. Such an examination evokes that of Propp in seeking to reveal the basic plot of the piece, its basic action units, though Propp's narrative map explores the contours of the tale in much greater detail. Does a description of generic elements of the tale together with a consideration of the work's stylistic features allow one to define the sort of literature it is, to make any suggestions about the producer and the receiver of the text?

Specific Elements

A next detailed level of description and classification outlines the "specific elements of content." In Genesis 12 the specification of the generic problem is the low status of the protagonists, the plan to solve the problem is a deception or an act of cleverness. At this level of analysis there are still numerous ways to fill in the steps—various sorts of conditions of low status or various sorts of deception—but the possibilities are fewer than in the generic analysis. Does this more detailed analysis provide further information? Do the specific elements of content arranged in particular ways lead to defining a morphology?[19] Having defined a set of specific elements that combine to form the morphology of the tale, one can proceed to inner-Israelite and cross-cultural comparison. Is this morphology a universal one? Does it underline certain basic human concerns?

Typological Elements

Another page on the narrative overlay is pulled down to describe the tale in more precise terms. The heroes can be identified as a husband and wife, the deception is to say the wife is a sister. These are to be called typological elements of content, the combination of which present a type in the style of Stith Thompson. At Thompson's level of description the story is pretty much told—the particular story—though names of the husband, wife, and foreign ruler need to be provided, and so on. Now one is able more closely to approach author-audience and sociohistorical questions. Does this particular rendering of a more general morphology help better to understand the meanings and messages of the piece, its role in the lives of a particular group?

Individual Elements

Finally, one moves to a further degree of specificity, to the nominal or individual level. The husband is Abram, the foreign setting, Egypt, and so on. Are these nuances significant in a fuller understanding of the work?

Text and Style in Three Tales

Genesis 12:10–20

There was a famine in the land, and Abram went down to Egypt to dwell because the famine was severe in the land. [11]And it happened when he approached Egypt he said to Sarai his wife, "Behold, now, I know that you are a beautiful woman. [12]When the Egyptians see you, they will say, 'This is his wife' and kill me and let you live. [13]Please say you are my sister so that it may go well with me because of you and my life be preserved on your account." [14]And it happened when Abram arrived in Egypt, the Egyptians saw the woman, that she was very beautiful. [15]The courtiers of Pharaoh saw Sarai, praised her to Pharaoh, and the woman was taken to Pharaoh's palace. [16]And he made it go well with Abram because of her, and he came to possess sheep and cattle and asses and slaves and maid-servants and she-asses and camels. [17]But Yahweh struck Pharaoh and his household with great plagues because of Sarai, the wife of Abram. [18]And Pharaoh called to Abram and said, "What is this you have done to me? Why did you not tell me that she is your wife? [19]Why did you say, 'She is my sister,' so that I took her for myself as a wife? And now here is your wife. Take her and go." [20]And Pharaoh assigned men to him and sent him away, and his wife, and all that was his.

Text-critically, Genesis 12:10–20 offers few problems.[20] We move ahead to matters of style. The composer of Genesis 12:10–20 uses language in a particularly skilled way. The slow pace of travel is conveyed by the elongated quality of 12:11, which in succinct English could be translated "when he approached Egypt" but in the halting Hebrew idiom actually says, "when he came near to coming to Egypt." The author could have employed briefer idioms but does not. The author is stylistically self-conscious. Similarly, Pharaoh's consternation with Abram after the revelation of the hero's relationship to Sarai is beautifully conveyed by brief staccato questions that wait for no answer. "What is this you have done? Why did you not tell me she is your wife? Why did you say, 'She is my sister,' so that I took her for myself as a wife?" (12:18–19). The brevity of the language at the end of verse 19 similarly conveys anger and the summary fashion in which Abram is dismissed. "And now here is your wife. Take her and go." The Hebrew *qaḥ wālēk*, "take and go," requires no repetition of the object and is even more quickly paced than the English.

A broader examination of the tale reveals an economical style. The term *economical* refers not to the frequently encountered terseness of classical Hebrew prose but to the fact that more often than not the same thought, image, or event is expressed in similar language throughout the narrative. This sort of economy, or to use A. B. Lord's term "thrift,"[21] emerges in the repeated language of 12:11–13, Abram's request and explanation to Sarai; of 12:14–16, the indication that events go exactly as planned; and in 12:19, Pharaoh's interrogation of Abram concerning the latter's scheme.

The essence of the story is thus reiterated in essentially similar language three times at key junctures in the narrative. These repetitions underline important motifs in the story, the setting in a strange land, the beauty of the wife, the wife-as-sister deception, a stranger's taking her to wife, and the success of the true husband. Such repetitions unify the narrative simply by reminding the reader of the heart of the matter, combining and recombining to create major stages in the plot. More subtly, they emphasize important directions and nuances in the tale. The very plan to save the hero's life and better his situation ("Please say you are my sister," 12:12–13) becomes the revelation by Pharaoh that leads to a new reduction in status for the hero, a new problem ("Why did you say, 'She is my sister'?" 12:18–19). The language that doubly emphasizes Abram's hoped for and realized success for himself and his family—"that it may go well with me because of you" (12:13), "and he made it go well with Abram because of her" (12:16)—first ironically contrasts with the singly mentioned plagues suffered by Pharaoh's household and then even more ironically with Abram's own ignominious departure from Pharaoh.

Hermann Gunkel suggests condescendingly that such economical style "originated in the poverty of language."[22] To the contrary, it is a sign of special skill in composition, an indication of a professional style, something set apart from ordinary patterns of speech. Economical style is, of course, one of the marks of oral composition, but one cannot leap to an assertion that Genesis 12:10–20 was orally composed. The presence of repetition is not proof enough. Genesis 12:10–20, however, is traditional in style, exhibiting a use of language common to skilled narrators of folktale.

Genesis 20:1–18

Abraham journeyed from there to the land of the south. He dwelled between Kadesh and Shur and sojourned in Gerar. ²And Abraham said concerning Sarah, his wife, that she was his sister, and Abimelech, king of Gerar, sent and took Sarah away. ³And God came to

Abimelech in a dream that night saying to him, "Behold you are a dead man because of the woman you took away, for she is a married woman." [4]But Abimelech had not approached her [sexually] and said, "My Lord, would you kill even a righteous man? [5]Did he himself not say to me, 'She is my sister,' and even she herself said, 'He is my brother'? I did this with integrity and innocence." [6]And God said to him in the dream, "I myself know that you did this with integrity, for I myself prevented you from sinning against me. For this reason I did not allow you to touch her. [7]But now return the man's wife, for he is a prophet and will pray for you so that you live. If you do not return [her] know that you will surely die, you and all who belong to you." [8]Abimelech rose early in the morning, called together all his servants, and told them everything, and the men feared greatly. [9]So Abimelech called to Abraham and said to him, "What have you done to us? How have I sinned against you that you have brought upon me and upon my kingdom a great sin? Things which are not done you have done to me." [10]And Abimelech said to Abraham, "What did you encounter that made you do this thing?" [11]Abraham said, "It was because I said to myself there is surely no fear of God in this place and they will kill me on account of my wife. [12]And truly she is my sister. She is my father's daughter but not my mother's daughter, and she became my wife. [13]It happened when God caused me to wander from my homeland I said to her, 'This is how you might show your devotion to me. Everyplace where we go say for me, 'He is my brother.' " [14]Then Abimelech took sheep and cattle, slaves and maidservants and gave them to Abraham, and he returned to him Sarah, his wife. [15]And Abimelech said, "Here is my land before you. Dwell wherever is good in your eyes." [16]And to Sarah he said, "Behold I am giving one thousand pieces of silver to your brother. Behold it is compensation for you. To all who are with you and with all things you are justified." [17]Then Abraham prayed to God, and God healed Abimelech and his wife and his female slaves so they could give birth, [18]for God had shut up every womb in Abimelech's household because of Sarah, wife of Abraham.[23]

Genesis 20 presents a few minor text-critical problems (as indicated in note 23). The style of Genesis 20 differs significantly from that of Genesis 12. Absent is traditional-style repetition whereby whole phrases recur at important narrative intervals with expected variations in subject, object, tense or the like (e.g., *lm'n yytb ly b'bwrk*, "so that it may go well with me because of you" [Gen. 12:13] versus *wl'brm hytyb b'bwrh*, "and he made it go well with Abram because of her" [Gen 12:16]). Genesis 20 includes some brief cases of repetition. Abraham's pronouncement concerning Sarah, "She is my sister" (20:2), is repeated in Abimelech's defense of himself to God. Abimelech precisely quotes Abraham's own words, thereby laying all blame upon him, "Did he himself not say to me, 'She is my sister?' " (20:5). The phrase "she is my sister" is not found in Abimelech's speech to Abraham, though it is echoed with interesting nuance and variation in syntax in Abraham's rationalization at 20:12, "Truly [she is] my sister" (*'mnh 'hty*). Repetition is also found in verses 5 and 6. Abimelech tells God, "I did this with integrity," and God repeats, "I know you did this with integrity." This repetition certainly serves to emphasize Abimelech's innocence but does not unify the narrative or direct it in significant directions. Here, in contrast to the style of Genesis 12, repetition is not really a compositional tool. The echo, "she is my sister," "truly my sister," has some dramatic effect, but there are not very many other ways to express this bit of content, and for the most part when feasible the author of Genesis 20 seems to prefer varied ways of expressing the same piece of content rather than similar ways.

For example, Abimelech's not consummating the marriage with Sarah is described in verse 4 as "he did not approach [*qrb*] her." Implicit is a lack of volition on his part or immediate opportunity. However, God's words in verse 6 provide stronger language to explain the unconsummated marriage. "I did not allow you to touch [*lng'*] her." Variation in language can, of course, be as effective and creative a compositional device as repetition. In this example, what at first seems to have been a choice of Abimelech or a matter of chance is seen to have been all along the result of firm divine control.

One technique of repetition is found in Genesis 20, a rhetorical device. A verb appears in two phrases, the second appearance in some way contrasting with or coloring the first usage. Note the variation between verses 7 and 14, 17: "but now return the man's wife . . . , [he] will pray for you so that you live" (20:7); "he returned to him Sarah, his wife" (20:14); "then Abraham prayed to God, and God healed Abimelech" (20:17). God's statements are the more general and the more sweeping, as befitting the deity, the narrator's voice more bound to the details of the situation. The same verb *return* or *pray* is thus employed in phrases of differing nuance to create a difference in voice, one that heightens the sense of a transcendent deity to be contrasted with the mundane and the human.

Another variety of this rhetorical device emerges in the composer's use of the verbs *fear* and *sin*. Abimelech's aides "fear greatly" when they hear of the king's dream (20:8). Abraham later says that he declared Sarah to be his sister because he felt "there is surely no fear of God in this place" (20:11). Abraham's excuse takes on a certain irony; the "fear" usages serve to emphasize the universality of fear of God. Even these foreigners recognize and respect his power and the truth of his words. "Sin" language appears in God's words to Abimelech in 20:6, "I myself prevented you from sinning against me," and in Abimelech's rebuke to Abraham at 20:9, "How have I sinned against you, that you have . . . ?" or "How I have sinned against you, for you have brought upon me and upon my kingdom a great sin?" Though God himself is able to declare he has prevented Abimelech from sinning, Abimelech—no matter which translation one prefers—with enormous scrupulousness, guilt, and recrimination against Abraham, declares himself to have sinned. Again his own strong sense of ethics, his "integrity of mind" is emphasized. This is the same man who returns the wife by precisely carrying out the command of verse 7, as the repetition in verse 14 indicates. This is the man whose innocence is emphasized by God's repetition of and endorsement of his own defense (see vv. 5 and 6).

Thus language is used in a rhetorically clever and skillful way in Genesis 20, but the rhetorical techniques are different from those of chapter 12. They employ a selective repetition that really is a form of variation in language rather than traditional economy or thrift.

Another important feature in Genesis 20 is the length of speeches by Abimelech and Abraham, this in contrast to the terse communications of hero and adversary in the account in Genesis 12.[24] Note, for example, Abimelech's defense to God in verse 5: "Did he himself not say to me . . . and even she herself said. . . . with integrity [literally, "with integrity of mind"] and innocence [literally, "with the innocence of my hands"]." There are briefer modes of speech. Contrast Pharaoh's brief and heated accusatory questions (12:18) and two-phrase overview of what has happened (12:19) with Abimelech's repetitions and wordy complaints, "What have you done to us? How have I sinned against you that you have brought upon me and upon my kingdom great sin? Things which are not done you have done to me" (20:9). Abraham's own explanation is a veritable soliloquy many lines long. No such explanation to the ruler is even found in Genesis 12. One is justified in speaking of a baroque style in Genesis 20, a fancier or more flowery style. This, combined with the composer's varied use of language and rather skilled rhetorical techniques, leads comfortably to suggestions of courtly composition.

Genesis 26:1–17

There was a famine in the land—aside from the former famine which was in the days of Abraham. And Isaac went to Abimelech, king of the Philistines, to Gerar. [2]And Yahweh appeared to him saying, "Do not go down to Egypt. Abide in the land as I tell you. [3]Sojourn in this land, and I will be with you and bless you, for to you and to your descendants I will give all these lands, and I will uphold the promise which I swore to Abraham your father. [4]And I will make your descendants as numerous as the stars of heaven and give to your descendants all these lands. In your descendants will be blessed all the peoples of the earth [5]because Abraham listened to my voice and kept my charge, commandments, statutes, and laws." [6]And Isaac dwelled in Gerar. [7]The men of the place asked about his wife, and he said, "She is my sister," because he was afraid to say, "She is my wife," [thinking] lest the men of the place kill me because of Rebecca, for she was beautiful. [8]And it happened after he had spent a long time there that Abimelech, king of the Philistines, was looking out the window and saw, lo and behold, Isaac at play with Rebecca his wife. [9]Then Abimelech called to Isaac and said, "Aha, she is your wife! How could you say, 'She is my sister?' " And Isaac said, "Because I said to myself, 'Lest I die because of her.' " But Abimelech said, "What is this you have done to us? What if one of the people had bedded your wife and brought upon us sin?" [11]Then Abimelech commanded all the people saying, "He who touches this man or his wife will surely die." [12]And Isaac sowed seed in that land and raked in one hundred-fold, for God blessed him. [13]So the man became wealthy, becoming more and more wealthy until he was exceedingly powerful. [14]He had flocks of sheep and herds of cattle and a great household, and the Philistines were jealous of him. [15]All the wells which his father's servants had dug in the days of Abraham his father the Philistines stopped up, filling them with earth. [16]Then Abimelech said to Isaac, "Leave us, for you are much stronger than we." [17]And Isaac went forth from there and camped in the valley of Gerar and dwelled there.

Once again, the Hebrew text offers no major difficulties. The style of Genesis 26:1–17, especially in the first five verses, is anthological; the author appears to reuse phrases found elsewhere in the tradition. It is always difficult to distinguish between the formula, a flexibly employed linguistic building block of the literary tradition, and the quotation, a direct reuse or borrowing of a phrase quite set in the tradition. Whether or not the author employs a traditional mode of interaction between the deity and the patriarch or quotes a now fixed Abraham tradition, the effect is to place the son in the light of the father and to create parallels between the experience of the father and that of the son. Thus 26:2, "And I will bless you," echoes 12:2. Note that the covenantal promise scene of chapter 12 precedes a wife-sister tale as in Genesis 26, but that in the latter the promise is an integrated part of the tale, the reason for staying in Gerar, where the experience with Abimelech takes place. "I will make your descendants as numerous as the stars of heaven" (26:4) is a clear echo of 22:17. "In your descendants will be blessed all the peoples of the earth" (26:4) echoes 12:3 and, more precisely, 22:18. The land promise of 26:3 echoes the language of 12:7 and the content of 22:17. All these linguistic connections, with their shared covenantal significance, have the effect of linking father-son experiences. Jacob, too, is told in language of land (ʾrṣ) and giving (ntn, verb) of the promise "to you and your descendants" (28:13). All the families of the earth will bless themselves by him and his descendants (Gen 28:14), and so the links, linguistic and covenantal, last for one more generation.

A less common phrase directly quotes 22:18 and explicitly evokes the experience of Abraham in the episode of the binding of Isaac. "because you listened to my voice" (22:18)—"because Abraham listened to my voice" (26:5). In a sense, Abraham's merits descend to Isaac. Because Abraham agreed to sacrifice Isaac, Isaac lives on to receive God's blessing and continue the tradition. The continuation of this quoted phrase at 26:4 and consequent nuance that attaches to it may provide a hint to the date of this composition: "and kept my charge, commandments, statutes, and laws." This is a chain popular in the Deuteronomic tradition (Deut. 11:1; 1 Kings 2:3—see 1 Kings 6:12 for variant). The phrase "to uphold or discharge the promise of" 26:3 (promise: šebūʿāh; uphold: hāqîm, causative of qwm, "to stand") is found only at Jeremiah 11:5 and may be an exilic period idiom, though this is not certain (see Lev. 26:9, 14; 1 Kings 6:12; Deut. 8:18; Jer. 2:20 for similar uses of hāqîm).

Note that God speaks in poetry, in heightened language of emphasis by nuance and repetition. As one reaches the wife-sister story itself a more ordinary prose medium reasserts itself. The covenantal scene and the following tale are linked by language of land-dwelling, abiding, and sowing. God tells the traveler, "Do not go down to Egypt. Abide in the land. . . . Sojourn in this land. . . . " (26:2). The patriarch "dwells in

Gerar" (26:6); he "sows in this land" (26:12). The land promise theme is a link in the tale as a whole. Also important is the use of "bless" in the opening interaction and the statement that God blesses Isaac later in the tale (26:12). The pattern of promise/fulfillment is strong in the very language of the piece. As it now stands, the covenantal scene and the tale of wife-assister are thoroughly interwoven. Stylistically, 26:12 ff. is an integrated continuation of God's actions on the patriarch's behalf in Gerar until the hero's departure at verse 17.

The author of Genesis 26:1–17 employs language to emphasize the distinction between the voice of God and the human voice. Genesis 26:1–17 exhibits neither the economy of language of Genesis 12:10–20 nor the elegance of Genesis 20. Certain repeated terms serve to echo key themes. Possibly exhibiting a preference for Deuteronomic and exilic usage, the author's style is anthological.

Conclusions

A study of wording and texture is enormously instructive. An economical traditional style in chapter 12 contrasts with a baroque style in chapter 20 and an anthological style in chapter 26. One cannot leap to the conclusion that the account in chapter 12 is orally composed; one should not leap to the conclusion that this account is necessarily earlier than the others. It is certain, however, that the authors of these variations on the wife-sister theme cannot be the same. Assignments of 12:10–20 and 26:1–17 to J fall apart, as does the insistence of Albright and others that J and E sources are indistinguishable, if one accepts the usual assignments of 12:10–20 and 20 to J and E.[25] What of Gunkel's suggestion that J and E were not authors, merely collectors, preserving earlier oral accounts?[26] Even the Brothers Grimm altered the style of the tales they collected to make them appeal to their nineteenth-century audiences.[27] Are we to believe that these collectors of the tenth, ninth, or eighth centuries B.C. preserved the style of tales with the precision of a modern folklorist? In any event, if J and E are merely collectors, they have no relevance to our study of folklore in context. What would have been the context of a Genesis 12:10–20 as narrated, not as collected? Old source theories cannot answer these questions. A study of the texture of these variants only begins to address questions concerning possible authors and audiences of the tales, but it seriously challenges their usual assignments to sources and indeed raises questions concerning the usefulness of the source theory itself as a means of understanding the meanings, functions, composition, transmission, and preservation of the various wife-sister narratives. Does the wording of the tales give evidence as to their relationship, to a transmission history they share?

As noted, the composer of Genesis 26:1–17 seems consciously to quote other materials of Scripture, alluding to the famine in Abraham's time that begins Genesis 12:10–20. This author, who quotes Genesis 22, nevertheless tells the wife-sister tale in many of his own words. Again, even this anthological author is to be regarded as a composer rather than a rote copier or an editor who cuts and pastes. Van Seters's view of a Genesis 20 that is based on Genesis 12 and a Genesis 26 based on chapters 12 and 20 is not upheld by an examination of language shared by the tellings.[28] The complaint of the ruler, "What [is this you] have you done to me/us?" found in Genesis 12:18; 20:9; and 26:10 is idiomatic language in biblical Hebrew to accuse a person of wrongdoing. (See Gen. 29:25, Jacob to Laban; Exod. 14:11, Israelites to Moses; Num. 23:11, Balak to Balaam; Judg. 8:1, Ephraimites to Gideon; Judg. 15:11, men of Judah to Samson.) The image of wealth expressed in a chain in 12:16 and 20:14 is a formulaic expression of wealth throughout Scripture (see Gen. 13:5; 24:35; 30:43; 1 Sam. 27:9; 2 Kings 5:27). The brief variations on the phrase "she is/you are my sister" present the simplest way to express this important bit of content, not evidence of copying. The ruler's admonition to the patriarch that he could have brought sin upon him or his household found in Genesis 20 and 26 shows variation in language (20:9; 26:10), so too the hero's expression of fear for his life as an excuse to the ruler 20:11; 26:9 (*hrg* vs. *mwt*),[29] though 26:7 and 20:11 share the phrase *hrg . . . 'l* ("kill me because of").

One cannot conclude that an ongoing process of rewriting characterizes the relationship between the three tales, when linguistic evidence for dependence is absent. Genesis 26:1–17 is later than Genesis 12:10–20, but the larger relative chronology suggested by Van Seters and Gunkel is not supported by the language of the accounts. Van Seters is correct to note that Genesis 20 and 26 are not oral-traditional in style. Genesis 12 is stylistically the most oral-traditional of the three, but one cannot easily draw conclusions about its oral composition. The persistence of key phrases such as "she is my sister" in these particular tales and of formulas like the possessions chain throughout Scripture, however, testifies to the traditional quality of much biblical writing. There are ways to express certain elements of content in a specific tale tradition and in the larger narrative tradition.

Evidence from the Overlay Map

Generic Elements

Moving to matters of structure with the overlay map as guide (see pp. 42–43), we find Genesis 12:10–20 to have a simple five-part structure (see "generic elements" on map). The action is "single-threaded" and unified; there are no subplots nor intertwining of various tales. Key events emerge in brief scenes, and characterizations are in bas-relief. Only the barest essentials in character motivation are provided, those necessary to move the plot from one stage of its structure to the next. Like John Van Seters's analysis, this description of the tale in Genesis 12 evokes Olrik's "epic laws of folktale."[30] The appeal of narratives with the generic characteristics displayed by Genesis 12:10–20 is universal and timeless. The tale's adherence to Olrik's laws does not aid in locating its setting or date to the extent suggested by some, but in part explains its popularity, its having been preserved. Though in some senses Genesis 12:10–20 is not sophisticated literature, it is rather sophisticated in others. That is, the ordinary person does not by nature tell stories in economical style or write in single strands. Such narratives are the stuff of storytellers, perhaps even trained professionals, those in a tradition of storytelling in a particular culture.[31]

In Genesis 20, an action by a character, unexplained and unmotivated, is followed by a second action or reaction by another. The complication that arises because of these motifs is synonymous with the problem of the tale. A brief plan to solve the problem is followed by a resolution in several parts, the details of which emerge in more detailed levels of analysis. This tale, even at the generic level, is implicitly more mysterious, more drama-building, and for this reason more complex than Genesis 12:10–20. It does not begin with a problem or "lack" in Proppian terms, but with an unexplained declaration.[32] The pace of the tale, as the stylistic analysis intimates, is rather swift until the problem is made apparent. A great deal of space is then alloted the scene in which the problem is made manifest and solutions suggested and carried out.

The reason for the opening action and a partial rationalization for it do not appear until after the complication/problem, five motifs into the story, whereas in Genesis 12 such an explanation is an intrinsic part of the opening problem motif, that which sets the story going. In two other instances (20:11–13, 18) important information about the characters' situations is withheld until unexpectedly late in the plot. The plot of Genesis 20 is more sophisticated than that of Genesis 12:10–20. The author controls information and pace in the tale with various interesting effects. Genesis 20 does not, in short, display the simple linear patterning found in traditional literature. The drama-creating, elongated generic pattern of events is an appropriate complement in content and structure to the baroque style described earlier. The composer creates articulate characters, employs pace effectively, and is not bound to the traditional ways of telling the story.

THE WIFE-AS-SISTER TALES: AN OVERLAY MAP

Style: Structure of Content:	Gen. 12:10–20 Economical	Gen. 20 Baroque-Rhetorical	Gen. 26:1–17 Anthological
Generic Elements	1. Problem 2. Plan 3. Execution 4. Complication 5. Outcome	1. Action 2. Reaction 3. Complication 4. Proposed Solution 5. Resolution	1. Problem 2. Intervention 3. Problem 4. Response 5. Complication avoided 6. Resolution 7. New Problem 8. Outcome
Specific Elements	1. Marginal status of protagonists 2. Deception/cleverness 3. Improved status of protagonists 4. Deception uncovered 5. Return to status as outsiders	1. Partial declaration by protagonist of state of affairs 2. Alteration of current order 3. Revelation that new order is in violation of proper order and threat to violator 4. To cancel the violation 5. Explanation/restoration of proper order	1. Marginal status of protagonists 2. Instructions/promise of improvement in status 3. Question perceived as threat 4. Deception 5. Deception uncovered 6. Heroes' lot improved 7. Confrontation 8. Return to status as outsiders
Typological Elements	1. Husband and wife face famine; become sojourners in a foreign land in search of food; husband fears he will be slain, his beautiful widow taken to wife by the aliens	1. "Wife is sister," announced to foreigners	1. Husband and wife face famine; unsureness concerning geographic decisions—to go or stay

	Gen. 12:10–20	*Gen. 20*	*Gen. 26:1–17*
	2. Husband has wife say she is his sister, "that it may go well"	2. "Sister" taken to harem of king (not married)	2. Divine helper advises heroes to stay and promises to take care of them
	3. "Sister" taken to ruler's palace as wife; ruler rewards "brother" with wealth	3. Divine revelation that sister is wife (wife is also sister). Death threat (actual illness) if wife not returned.	3. Foreigners ask, "Who is woman?"
	4. Brother found out to be husband because of a divine helper's intervention	4. To return the wife	4. Hero responds, "She is my sister."
	5. Husband and wife thrown out of town	5. Fear had been motivation. Wife is sister. Wife is returned. Compensation given. Healing. Remaining in kingdom	5. Wife is not sister. Ruler commands, "Do not touch."
			6. Wealth via helper's blessing
			7. Heroes asked to leave because they are "too mighty"
			8. Departure of heroes
Individual Elements	1. Abram and Sarai	1. Abraham declares to people of Gerar	1. Isaac and Rebecca in land of Gerar/Abimelech
		2. Ruler is Abimelech	2. Yahweh/convenantal form
	3. Pharaoh is ruler	3. God reveals in a dream	
	4. Yahweh brings plagues	4. God's suggestion to return Sarah confirmed by consultation with courtiers	
			5. Uncovering of deception by simple observation of the married couple's actions, not by divine intervention. Any possible threat to wife avoided.
			6. Planting/reaping. Success in "land" terms
			7. Jealousy—us/them

Genesis 26 presents yet another configuration of generic elements. The problem is partially addressed by the second motif in the pattern, awaiting full resolution in subsequent motifs. The second problem and the response do not initiate the plot, in contrast to the problem/plan and action/reaction of Genesis 12:10–20 and Genesis 20. The motifs of problem and response (nos. 3 and 4), moreover, are neutralized in motifs 5 and 6. The narrative patern of Genesis 26, described in generic terms, reveals a tale that never develops; problems and threats are counteracted before leading to complications. The plot is so tightly controlled that the tale as tale is not, in fact, very exciting.

Specific Elements

Genesis 12:10–20 and the Morphology of the Trickster

The first three specific elements of the five-part pattern reveal Genesis 12:10–20 to be an underdog tale, one that marks a progression from lower to higher status. This basic morphology applies to various tales in Thompson's Type-Index, stories such as "Cinderella" (type 510) or "The King and the Peasant's Son" (type 921), narratives about heroes and heroines who make their way with magical or human helpers or through their own wisdom or savvy. Such a morphology describes on a basic level many of the narratives to be examined here, for example, the tales of Joseph in Egypt, of Jacob at his father-in-law's, of Esther at the court of Ahasuerus. Type 922, which characterizes Genesis 41 and Daniel 2, is a specific working out of this same morphology.

Genesis 12 extends the three-part pattern of the "underdog" with two further steps that are specifications of the generic elements, complication and outcome: deception uncovered and reduction-of-status/return-to-status-as-outsiders. The tale is thereby rendered into a variety of the "underdog" morphology that in this study is called "the trickster." The raise in status for the heroes is followed by an unmasking of the plot, the deception, that helped them to achieve initial success. The plot revealed, the heroes' status is again reduced. The jig is up, but the protagonists survive to be involved in another plot, in the sense of both narrative and deception.

The term *trickster* is used by anthropologists and folklorists to describe a particular character who appears in the lore of various cultures, including those of West Africans and American Indians. Robert Pelton, commenting on the work of Daniel Brinton, describes the North American Indian trickster as "gross deceiver, crude prankster, creator of the earth, a shaper of culture, a fool caught in his own lies."[33] MacLinscott Ricketts suggests that "the trickster is man . . . struggling by himself to become what he feels he must become—master of his universe."[34] He is "noble and foolish, heroic and cowardly, daring and deceitful, often beaten but never defeated."[35] Paul Radin emphasizes the trickster's liminality, his "undifferentiated" quality (he is often pictured as a man/woman or human/animal), and his status as wanderer[36] and suggests that this traditional character is a creation of the common man rather than of priests and shamans,[37] an interesting suggestion recently challenged by Pelton's seminal study.[38] Deceiver, creator, acculturator, unmasked liar, survivor—these qualities of the trickster do apply to the deceiving, ethically ambiguous survivor Abram of Genesis 12:10–20. It is appropriate that this progenitor of the Israelites, traditional founder of Yahwism, first participant in the special covenant of one group with God, be portrayed as a trickster. He is a creator and a culture maker of sorts, though a much more sedate version of the bawdy hero who appears in various West African and American Indian tales. Admittedly, con man might be a more accurate designation.

In fact, the folktales of many cultures include just such a trickster, who is some steps removed from the mythological hero but still clearly in the same family. The Abram tale in Genesis 12 leads to the outline of a specific trickster morphology; that is, a specific pattern of narrative elements in which the trickster acts out his or her role.[39] This morphology, one finds, is not unique to Israelite literature but is found throughout the world.

A fine example of this morphology is found among the tales of the Winnebago Trickster Cycle.[40] The Trickster and his friends find themselves starving in a snowy winter. Trickster metamorphoses into a woman and in this disguise marries a chief's son, a successful hunter. All goes as planned for a time. Trickster, the man-woman, lives well and bears his/her husband three sons, but eventually the ruse is uncovered and Trickster runs away. (For the full text, see the appendix at the end of this chapter.) Similar versions of this tale are found among the Assiniboine Indians and are provided by Radin in summary.[41]

At first glance one might ask what these bawdy tales of changling, mythopoeic tricksters have to do with the tale of the patriarch and his wife. As Dundes shows so beautifully, though two tales may be distinguishable on the basis of function in a cultural community, in terms of setting in which they are told, and on the basis of content—that is, in the layers of content we distinguish as typological and individual—the tales may be identical in terms of morphological structure, that is, at the level of content we call specific.[42] One might on the basis of typological content, function, and setting wish to designate two tales as myth and folktale, but the myth and the folktale may well share the same morphological structure.

Stith Thompson's Type-Index includes a set of narratives under the heading, "The Clever Boy" (type 1542). These stories share our morphology: low status of heroes; deception planned to improve conditions; improved status; deception uncovered; reduction of status/survival. Following is the summary of a Norwegian tale, an interesting working out of this morphology.[43] This tale shares details with the Abram account on a level beyond the morphological, as does Thompson's outline of the type 1542.

A poor lad and his sister make their way in life through trickery. The hero dresses in his sister's clothing and fools the king into marrying him. When the ruse is uncovered, the king attempts to have the hero killed, but he escapes.

The *Odyssey* provides another example of a trickster morphology in one incident that is an important link in the larger narrative chain of the epic. In Book Nine, Odysseus tells of his capture and escape from the Cyclops Polyphemos. The reduced status of the heroes in the context of the narrative is their having become prisoners and, indeed, a source of food, mere edibles, for their unacculturated captor, who eats Achaians by the handful. The deception or trick designed by Odysseus is to make the Cyclops drunk, to blind him, and then escape tied to the monster's sheep as they leave his cave to reach pasture. A part of this clever scheme is to make the giant believe Odysseus' name is "Nobody." The hero, however, creates a complication for himself, unmasking a key part of his deception, when out of bravado he reveals his true identity to the injured son of Poseidon. In this way, once again, the heroes become prisoners of sorts, the prisoners of Poseidon; the men of Odysseus are to die at sea and he to suffer further wandering and statuslessness.

The same trickster morphology may thus emerge in an independent story, as in the Norwegian and Hebrew examples, or be woven into the fabric of a more complex narrative work, but the pattern of motifs is visible in all cases.

Recognition of this shared morphology is important, allowing one to deal in new ways with certain old questions about the wife-sister tale in Genesis 12. From a discussion of the general and the shared, one can then move on to Israel's own particularization of the morphology with greater insight. It is often asked how the patriarch Abram can be involved in a lie. The writer of Genesis 20, as noted by Samuel Sandmel,[44] was himself not comfortable in telling the story this way. The problem should, however, be posed differently. Abram of Genesis 12 succeeds via tricks because he is a trickster, but why does such a morphology appeal to an Israelite writer? Why would an underdog-trickster appeal to any audience?

The attraction of the simple three-part underdog tale is not difficult to explain. The underdog addresses one's feelings of insecurity and smallness, be they rooted in material or psychological causes. For this reason, underdog tales are found in every culture, though admittedly they so appealed to the Hebrew writers that they appear to dominate the narratives of Israelite heroes. Other models are available for leaders—noble princes, well-born warriors, the very sort of hero who appears in Genesis 14. It is tempting to suggest that Israelites saw themselves as perpetual underdogs, because of the historical circumstances of their origins, because of the ups and downs of their subsequent history. But why the appeal of the underdog-trickster who succeeds via schemes only to be found out?

Though the simple underdog morphology is a narrative form of wish fulfillment for its author and audience, the trickster variant comforts in a different way. In identifying with the trickster one is enabled better to accept one's fortunes as a given and to be assured that if one does not succeed one at least survives. Underdogs who are also tricksters have a certain bravado. They survive because they have the nerve to use their wits. They appeal also because they are so human in their sneakiness, their trickiness.[45]

Abram's bravado is more understated than that of an Odysseus, but is implicit. Though his assumption of the brother role is said to be motivated by fear, no comment accompanies the indication that Abram becomes wealthy "because of her." He plays his role, presumably, with complete, bare-faced equanimity. As in other examples of the trickster morphology, the audience is never tense about the hero's safety or concerned for the heroine's honor. The text's matter-of-fact tone, its calm pace, does not lead to such emotional reactions—this in contrast, for example, to the dramatic, tension-building tale of the binding of Isaac in Genesis 22. The deadpan quality of Genesis 12:10–20 is important. An Israelite would be predisposed to root for the Israelite trickster over the foreign overlord, but the antagonist here is more of a blusterer than a feared and despised enemy. Finally, there is little ethical value judgment in the tale. It is not entirely permissible to deceive, for the hero is found out and demoted. On the other hand, he leaves with his deceitfully acquired goods intact. The duped person, moreover, is not to be excused or commiserated with.

The trickster morphology has an antiestablishment quality at the very source of its being. In discussing the popularity of trickster tales among Afro-Americans, Jay D. Edwards writes: "They capture and express the social and moral dilemmas of people living under conditions of enforced political and economic marginality."[46]

Success is achieved in an irregular, roundabout way, by deception, a trick. Edwards notes further that trickster tales involve the choice between adopting the value system of the dominant society or "maximizing short-term gain," which is "a dilemma inherent . . . to a considerable extent in the world of every socialized human being."[47] I do not suggest that all trickster tales appeal only to fringe people in a culture, for all humans, even those in "establishments," have a rebel side. Trickster tales do have general appeal; however, one would expect such tales to have special meaning and resonance for those not part of the establishment.

The tale's rather untroubled attitude about the success and setbacks of its heroes, its lack of ethical value judgment, its lack of polemic against the antagonist, make it very difficult to suggest that the composer of this tale is a theologically sensitive court writer during the nationalistic imperial heyday of Judaea, the description assigned to the Yahwist, who is usually regarded as the source of this tale. Can one suggest that "J," the Yahwist, merely preserved the tale intact and that it comes from a different period or a different immediate environment than his own?[48] Perhaps, but then the "sources" become irrelevant for our interest in genuine authors and audiences.

The tale would seem to provide the greatest power of identification to those not at the center of power, those unconcerned indeed with "the State" as such. The attitude to God implicit in this tale awaits a next level of analysis, but even on the morphological level, one does not anticipate a God who upholds ethical mores or rewards proper behavior. "J," supposed source of the flood account and of the Eden narrative, is imagined to have such attitudes; such a writer is not at work here.

Genesis 20 and the Status Quo

The morphological structure of Genesis 20 is designed to create surprises. A slow and ordinary beginning leads to unexpected reversals and twists but ultimately to a return to the opening situation and to a revelation that the actor and the reactor in the narrative, on some level, were both "right," both violators and violated. In a sense the plot of the tale is quite circular. The heart of the morphology is the pattern violation-of-order/threat-to-violator/restoration-of-order. Is the trickster characterization appropriate here, for the essence of trickster narratives is a breaking down of proper orders? This tale evokes the trickster; one is reminded of the riddle that only Samson, a trickster, can solve, the unfair, nonriddle riddle based on his own observation of a swarm of honeybees in the carcass of the lion he had killed. So too this hero's riddle: How is a seeming declaration both true and untrue so that it leads someone else to become a violator while one remains honest oneself? There is no doubt that the essence of Genesis 20, like that of Genesis 12, evokes the trickster, with its "wrong" configurations of relationships based on misinformation (cf. examples of type 1542, the king who takes Peik dressed as a woman to wife).

There are important differences, however. First, characters of the tale do not undergo an improvement and/or subsequent reduction in social status, such alterations in status being important fixtures of the trickster morphology found in Genesis 12. Genesis 20 emphasizes the maintenance of proper order in the social relationships between characters of the tale, the violation of this order, and its restoration. The tale's interest ultimately is in the status quo; it ends in resolution, harmony, and restoration; all is as it was. The disruption of a state of equilibrium is, in fact, the central problem of the tale. The reason for the hero's opening declaration, which sets the scene for subsequent events, is only a loose end, neatened in the final resolution motif. Stylistic interest in dramatic effect only explains, in part, the placement of the hero's explanation. The further effect of this narrative arrangement is to make the hero's status—lowly or princely or lowly again—much less an issue. The central problem of the tale is not that of the initial actor but that of the person who reacts to him, who unwittingly creates a state of disequilibrium. Interwoven in the pattern of order/violation-of-order/restoration-of-order is the submotif (indicated in parentheses on map) of the deception that turns out to be partial truth. Though the deception/nondeception contributes to the tale's dramatic style, it also contributes to the central themes of order/disorder. A nagging source of imbalance—the discontinuity between the hero's statement and the facts—is avoided.

The complex and sophisticated morphological design of Genesis 20 and the emphasis on status quo, combined with the baroque style of the narrative, contrast sharply with the trickster tale of Genesis 12. Genesis 20 is not as "traditional" a tale as Genesis 12:10–20 and seems less an underdog tale than the other versions; it is the least morphologically assignable to that category. Such a tale is more imaginable in a court setting, produced for members of the establishment.

Genesis 26:1–17, An Underdog Tale with Deception on the Side

Genesis 26, like Genesis 12, traces a pattern from marginal status to improvement indicative of the underdog tale. Also found is the deception and the deception uncovered, often the mark of the trickster. A direct question is the way in which the perceived threat is specified; the deception is a response to the threat, a way of dealing with it. In contrast to Genesis 12, where the deception leads to the heroes' improvement and the uncovering to their reduction in status, the uncovering of the deception in Genesis 26 precedes the improvement in the heroes' status. The arrangement of specific elements in Genesis 26 thus presents an underdog tale but not necessarily a trickster tale. Marginality is replaced with an improvement in status, the deception cluster being a minor source of drama along the way.

Some Conclusions from Morphological Study

An analysis of the three tales at the level of specific elements introduces the morphologies of the underdog and the trickster, patterns that underlie all the tales in our study. At this level, cross-cultural comparison becomes possible, as do certain sociological and psychological questions pertaining to the multiple meanings the tales may have held for a range of Israelite authors and audiences.

This approach to the wife-sister tales provides important information about the workings of biblical narrative. First, the tales in Genesis 12, 20, and 26 are not all equally traditional in the technical sense in which we have employed the term. Their range in terms of morphology is Genesis 12:10–20, most traditional, Genesis 26:1–17, next, and Genesis 20, least traditional. Second, we have raised questions about assignments to J and E in the case of these three tales and, third, about source theory in general.

The specific level of analysis has also taught much about the workings of all narrative, exploring (1) the way in which a very general pattern, for example, problem/resolution, can be specified in particular morphologies (Gen. 12:10–20 and Gen. 26:1–17) and (2) the way that the same important specific element, for example, deception, can make for a quite different story depending on where it appears in relation to the other specific elements.

The Typological Level

Genesis 12:10–20

The protagonists of Genesis 12:10–20 are a married couple, their marginality defined by a condition of famine. The search for food brings them to a foreign land and fear of its people, the specific fear being that the husband will be killed and the wife usurped. The deception that is chosen would seem to provide not only a means of coping with the fear of being killed but also a means of integrating the wanderers into their new environment in a more accepted, settled way. The man has the wife agree to say she is his sister, "that it may go well with him." It does. The ruler of the land takes her to wife, providing the "brother" with wealth. The wanderers' state of famine and marginality seems overturned. Once the plan is uncovered by the ruler, however, the pair are thrown out of town, though they leave with their wealth intact. The uncovering of the deception involves a helper who makes the ruler fear to have the trickster about.

The famine, though a common motif in the Hebrew Scriptures and a frequent reason for a change in setting, is a universal marker of marginality, the absence of sustenance being a deep-rooted and most basic human problem, the provision of food understandably the mark of blessing.

The foreign setting and the foreignness of the antagonists are also familiar underdog situations, though exilic status is of special interest and frequency in biblical tales and may have held special appeal for Israelite authors and audiences, whose very founding myths tell of departure from an original homeland and subsequent enslavements abroad.

The wife-as-sister deception is an unusual one. As the tales about Jacob show, there are other ways for an underdog to trick his way to success. E. A. Speiser's famous suggestion that this motif reflects real-life Hurrian marriage custom whereby the husband adopts his wife as sister has been rejected by the consensus of contemporary scholars.[49]

In non-Israelite examples of the trickster morphology, tricks often involve sexual disguise—common tricks in folktales being the male's assumption of female dress to attract a duped, wealthy suitor or the female's disguise in male clothing to attract the king's son.[50] Is not the wife-as-sister disguise another form of sexual or marriage trick? Indeed, Laban as trickster performs another variation on this trick when he passes off the unattractive Leah as the beautiful and beloved Rachel on the hero's wedding night. There are, however, additional dimensions to the act of deception as employed in this Israelite tale.

Having the protagonists be husband and wife and the antagonist a threat to the life of the male partner sets up an especially effective us-them dichotomy. The little family is a whole, some source of security in an insecure situation. The transformation of the wife into a temporary sister via deception appears to be an attempt to maintain family cohesion while obtaining the means of overcoming the family's difficulties. In fact, however, the heroes end up exchanging one sort of marginality for another. Abram remains a marginal person, whether a wanderer facing starvation or a brother-in-law to the king, for his status rests upon the unsolid ground of deception. This deception is guaranteed to continue his ambiguous status, to keep things out of joint.

Scholars have long noted certain ethical inconsistencies in the tale and wondered about God's role. First, the hero is pictured assuming that the foreigners would not take a married stranger's wife, but would prefer murder to adultery. Even more interesting is the antagonist's scolding of the hero, "Why did you not tell me that she is your wife?" (12:18). There is a clear attitude of opposition to adultery here, but also an assumption that all people are subject to this antiadultery commandment, even kings—perhaps especially kings. Recall Samuel's warning about the women-stealing tendencies of kings in 1 Samuel 8 and, more specifically, the case of David and Bathsheba. In Genesis 12, a foreign monarch is shown to be more fastidious than the Judaean king.

Secondly, the one who is punished is not the trickster but the monarch who commits adultery. In some sense, marriage to the foreigner does not count as the real thing; it is an acceptable means to an end, and one is led to believe that the hero would have remained in this situation of newly acquired status, content forever, had his scheme not been uncovered. The would-be helper, in fact, becomes the spoiler. The way the plan is uncovered and by whose intervention turns this tale into religious literature.

Genesis 20

It is on the typological level that one becomes most conscious of what Genesis 20 shares with Genesis 12:10–20. The wife-sister motif is present, as is the taking of the woman, the revelation of her true identity, and her return. Once again the wife is declared to be a sister, but the reason for this seeming deception is buried deep within the resolution of the tale, a part of the denouement rather than of the opening motivation. The hero, moreover, explains that the woman is indeed his half sister; they have made public only one side of their family relationship as a precaution throughout their travels. Thus the deception is not really a deception.

It might be suggested that the author of Genesis 20 portrays Abraham as an even more subtle con man than does the author of Genesis 12; he deceives by telling the truth or half-truth. However, the declaration that Sarah is his half sister comes at a point of genuine heart-baring by Abraham, a prelude to resolution in the tale. This declaration, along with the hero's description of his inner fears and motivations, is designed to create sympathy for the hero, a hero so scrupulous that even a deception planned in self-defense is a partial truth.

The wife-sister motif is altered in an important way when the husband and wife genuinely are the children of one father, half siblings. Several scholars argue that, on some level, Abraham's incestuous relationship with Sarah would have been regarded in a negative light by biblical writers. It seems clear that the author of Genesis 20 displays no such self-consciousness, the relationship between the protagonists providing a positive cast to the hero's character; that is, his opening words to the people of Gerar technically are all true. James G. Williams contributes an important clue to the significance of the wife-sister motif when he notes that incestuous relations are attributes of "royal" or "godly" couples, for example, Cronos and Rhea, Siegmund and Sieglinde.[51] Thus on the typological level one sees that the author of Genesis 20 seeks to portray the heroes as "high class"—as royalty, equal to their counterpart in Gerar and deserving of the latter's large financial settlement for their trouble.

The portrayal of the monarch in this tale is as interesting as the portrayal of husband and wife. He is scrupulously honest. The divine being directly reveals the truth to this person. The effect, as in Genesis 12, is to show the foreigner's implicit fear of God. The character who should be playing the role of adversary plays a veritable patriarchal role in his close and positive relationship with the divine. Implicit here is a certain respect for people such as Abimelech who are in positions of power, a respect that is not grudging or implicitly mocking but genuine. It is also significant that he is a non-Israelite. Such people are capable of deserving respect, human and divine. As noted in the morphological analysis, the should-be "adversary" in Genesis 20 is the victim, his problem and its rectification a focus of the tale equally important to the focus on the hero and his wife. This is a tale without a villain.

The woman-taking motif is also of special note. The "taking" is to be understood as a literal transporting of her person, not a euphemism for consummation of the marriage. As in character portrayals of the hero and his adversary, a "squeaky cleanness" is attached to the "wife stealing" itself. Nothing happens conjugally, according to narrator, Abimelech, and God (Gen. 20:4–6). The author here contrasts with the earthier composer of the trickster tale in Genesis 12.

Finally, note the many-faceted resolution motif composed of (1) the hero's explanation of his actions, (2) the actual returning of the woman, (3) the accompanying compensation in goods to the husband and money for the wife ceremonially given, (4) the healing, (5) the remaining in the land. The author is concerned with tying up all loose ends, this in contrast to the author of Genesis 12, who never explains, for example, how Pharaoh understands the meaning of the plagues. The ceremoniousness of Abimelech's act of compensation is noteworthy: verse 16 has a rather legal, even covenantal quality. The hero's gain is genuine compensation and not ill-begotten goods from a successful trickster's ploy. The king refers to the hero as the woman's brother in verse 16, an implicit reminder that the hero never lied. Finally, the tale ends with an invitation to the hero and his wife-sister to remain in the kingdom and enjoy its bounty. How different this conclusion from the summary dismissal of the heroes in Genesis 12! The heroes of Genesis 20 remain in a position of strength and confidence.

An examination of typological motifs further strengthens the impression of a courtly writer of the kind imagined in a J or E. The heroes are portrayed as royalty; respect for authority is strong; morality is conventional; the ethics of hero and foreign counterpart above reproach; the tale itself neat as a pin.

Genesis 26:1–17

Genesis 26:1–17, like Genesis 12:10–20, begins with famine, but includes the related problem of whether or not to leave the present geographic location in search of food. What better manifestation of rootlessness and insecurity? The advice of the divine helper to stay and the promise of help are fulfilled in the resolution, wealth obtained through the helper's blessing. These divine help motifs are key movers in the tale's plot, as noted at the specific level. With more detail now visible at the typological level, one sees that the wife-sister motifs are nonessential to the plot. They are not a route to wealth as spoils of a trick or as compensation for lost honor. Martin Noth suggests that this version of the three is the most "profane."[52] In fact, this version is the most heavily theological, reliant as its plot is on the foreground participation of a divine helper. The wife-sister motifs must have been favorites familiar in Israel; here they lenghten and enhance the tale with an adventure, but they are not major movers of the plot concerning the success of the divine helper's protégé. Note that the heroine is never taken in any sense by a foreigner. When contrasted with the other accounts, Genesis 26:1–17 exemplifies the way in which motifs that are thematically central in one tale may provide entertaining, supportive, but noncentral material in another. Whereas the story line of Genesis 12 is husband and wife trick Pharaoh out of wealth by convincing him that the wife is an eligible sister, the story line of Genesis 26 is husband and wife succeed by protection and blessing of a divine donor.

Finally, a comment on characterization: the adversary of Genesis 26 is as scrupulous as that of Genesis 20 but is much more sketchily drawn. The heroes' powerlessness clearly contrasts with the omnipotence of their divine helper. As he assumes the foreground, the roles of human protagonists and antagonists as movers of the plot fade.

Some Conclusions from Typological Study

This level of analysis has led to an examination of the cultural and psychological resonances of certain motifs, the wife-as-sister deception and famine as marginality. We have explored the implicit attitudes to secular power and authority, a sociological issue, and degrees of divine presence, a theological issue. At this level, characterization in the tales is described in more detail: the con artist of Genesis 12 versus the fastidious hero of Genesis 20 versus the divine helper's protégé in Genesis 26; and the divine helper, very much more in the foreground in Genesis 26 than in Genesis 12. At the typological level one can, in a line, report the essence of each story. The motif that is critical to one tale, a central theme, may be in another tale incidental music or accompaniment.

Although the accounts in Genesis 12, 20, and 26 hold motifs

in common, variations in their positioning and nuance lead to three quite different tales, tales that would come from different sorts of authors and be composed for different sorts of audiences. The categories popular, courtly, and homiletical are working designations for these contextual differences. We next explore a final level of specificity and then put all the findings together.

The Individual Level

Genesis 12:10–20

The husband and wife in Genesis 12:10–20 are the patriarch Abram and his wife, Sarai. The tale becomes especially significant when attached to these first ancestral heroes. Though modern readers might be tempted to suggest that Sarai is treated like a mere possession—more old-fashioned ones, that Sarai is willing to sacrifice herself for her husband—the language of the account suggests that Abram relates to Sarai lovingly and implies that they undertake the trick together. Abram praises his wife, "You are a beautiful woman" (12:11). He asks for cooperation and does not demand. "Please say you are my sister" (12:13). One has to assume that Sarai is his tacit accomplice, an Olrik's "twin" to Abram, a narrative equivalent to him.

The setting Egypt is also interesting. Though Egypt is a traditional place for refuge during famines, its association in this tale with the heroes' acquired riches and their hasty departure surrounded by hostility surely evokes the exodus. The evocation of exodus is further conveyed by the plagues that lead to the heroes' being sent forth. The monarch is Pharaoh, but how different his portrayal than that of the Pharaoh in Exodus. The Pharaoh of Genesis 12 is a scolding, offended party who has been duped. The only bitterness in this account, the only sense of indignation, is Pharaoh's. Some of the differences between this account and the exodus account have to do with their being different genres. The writer of Genesis 12 maintains a psychological distance from the Egyptians, allowing for a fairly comic portrayal.

God's role as helper/rescuer can be viewed as that of a spoiler. God waits until the hero becomes rich before interrupting the plot. God is the power behind the tale, the tricksters' controller. He neatens and organizes; his preferences define protagonists and antagonists and are to be identified with those of the writer.

There is a silence in this story. How does Pharaoh know that the plagues have to do with Sarai's unacceptability as a wife? Foreign or new women are always suspect, as indicated by the marriage problems of Tobit's future daughter-in-law and Judah's hesitation to give more sons to Tamar (Genesis 38), but Pharaoh actually states that he has come to realize that Sarai is Abram's wife and that the adultery is the cause of his problems. Has something been left out? This tale was, no doubt, a common and popular one, and the passage from initial success to uncovering was expected, waited for. Such is the power of traditional narrative patterns. The inevitability of God's will and the predictability of the folktale pattern thus reinforce one another.

Genesis 20

The person of high status in Genesis 20 is Abimelech of Gerar, a local petty tyrant who contrasts with the powerful Pharaoh of Genesis 12. Such a choice for the role of king in the tale places the Israelite heroes on a more equal footing with the foreign monarch and serves to heighten their status in the context of the story.

God reveals the problem to Abimelech in a dream, and following the dream Abimelech consults his courtiers. The bad-dream/consultation-with-courtiers cluster is found in various court tales, such as those about Joseph and Daniel (note the use of the formula *wayyiqrā' lĕkol*, "and he called to all . . . [names of court officials]"). The importance of kings' dreams in ancient Near Eastern courtly genres of fiction and nonfiction is well recognized.[53] Certainly any folktale teller can and does employ royal scenery. The case could be made that such consultations are what ordinary people expect in a courtly scene. Nevertheless, the dream/consultation details combine with other stylistic, morphological, and typological features to give an impression of a writer at home in courtly culture, one concerned that the story reflect that culture, and so it does in style, sensibilities, and details of content.

Genesis 26:1–17

Genesis 26:1–17 includes Isaac and Rebecca as heroes. The divine helper is Yahweh, who makes his appearance in a clearly covenantal form. Success of the heroes is in "land" terms of planting and reaping, the munificence of the Deuteronomic blessings. The covenantal component is much more overt in this wife-sister tale than in the others. Another detail that sets this account apart from the others is the ordinary way in which the deception is uncovered, through the ruler's observation of a romantic interlude between Rebecca and Isaac.

Conclusions

The overlay map analysis of Genesis 12:10–20; Genesis 20; and Genesis 26:1–17 is undeniable confirmation that folklore is helpful in the study of biblical narrative. The layered structuralist approach influenced by Propp, Dundes, Jason, and others allows one to explore closely the content, form, and meaning of each narrative and to compare the three versions on various narrative levels. We have learned that having several typological motifs in common does not necessarily mean stories have the same morphology and that stories of the same morphology may well be significantly different at the typological level. Cross-cultural comparison has been critical in discovering the Abram of Genesis 12 as a trickster and the various implications of that universal type for appreciating the tale. Folklorists' emphases on texture have interwoven with the rhetorical criticism of Bible scholars; old source-critical and redaction-critical assumptions have been challenged by an orientation toward performance by authors for audiences, notions of life-setting nuanced by anthropological and sociological bents. Rather than lead us directly to a relative chronology for the three accounts or a redaction history for each, the overlay map leads to suggestions about relative traditionality, relative self-consciousness about matters theological, and relative degrees of respect for authority expressed in each narrative. Multiple layers of content and structure function at once to render each narrative meaningful.

Can we set each of these tales in context? Unlike folklorists dealing with lore in process, we cannot assess the cultural and sociological context of the tale production directly. The tales themselves must be our informants. Do the worldview and ethos expressed in them tally with what we believe we know about Israelite history? What is the internal evidence for the tales?

Genesis 12:10–20 is in the style of traditional narrative, its generic elements simple and straightforward, its morphology that of a universal form of trickster tale, and its antiestablishment bent and breezy attitude toward its heroes' ethics appropriate to this morphology. The constellation of individual elements (Pharaoh/Egypt, plagues, hasty departure) leads one to conclude that it was composed after the formation of the Exodus tradition, providing an allusion in a trickster tale to the weightier epic. Its lack of bitterness toward foreign monarchs and particularly toward Egypt itself may imply this piece comes from a period of relative security, certainly from a period in which exodus and conquest are a part of the past integrated into a literary *topos*.

A comparison between Genesis 12 and 20 raises interesting questions about the workings of narrative content and structure and about the transformational capacities of narrative. The comparison also leads to some new suggestions about the composers of biblical narrative. The underdog-trickster tale in Genesis 12 and its not-quite-underdog relative in Genesis 20 point to two different sorts of authors. The latter has a marked interest in the high status and fine moral qualities of the heroes and ultimately tells a tale about the threat to the status quo and its restoration. The linguistic style is baroque, the narrative structures complex. The author presents courtly details and rather ceremonious interactions between characters. The morality is veritably "middle class," for the author emphasizes the truthfulness of the hero, the abiding purity of the heroine, and the innocence of the royal adversary. Emphases in the tale are on restoration of proper relationships between people and God and on healing. The hero's gain is merely due compensation, that which publicly sets matters aright. All this leads one to be most comfortable with the usual suggestions that Genesis 20 was written by a court writer during a healthy monarchic period (tenth through eighth centuries B.C., northern or southern). Genesis 12 could not be a composition of the same author.

Theologically, there are subtle differences among the tales. The deity of Genesis 20 speaks to the human king in a dream, omniscient, omnipotent, but understanding. In Genesis 12, God, though powerful, appears only in the wings, as plague sender. He is the trickster's helper and the barely mentioned controller of the plot. In Genesis 20 God becomes the spokesman for restoration. One cannot avoid thinking of covenant in reading God's complaint to Abimelech. The proper set of relationships has been violated; punishment will follow unless restitution is made. Abimelech is told to ask Abraham to intervene with prayer, a role in which he is found in Genesis 18, but here Abraham is actually called a prophet. The patterns of thought reflected in the tale are overtly more covenantal, more theologically self-conscious, than those of Genesis 12. This theological self-consciousness is again in tune with scholarly assumptions about courtly writers, their roles and interests.

Genesis 26:1–17, an underdog tale, concentrates more on the divine helper and the reliability of his promise than upon wife-sister motifs. With an even greater covenantal emphasis than Genesis 20, reflected not only in the structure of motifs at all levels but also in the very language of the piece, Genesis 26 is the most heavily theological of the three.

Except for 26:1 ff. Isaac has no adequate scene of covenant making with God. In fact, this tale is his Genesis 12 and Genesis 22 in one, with its promises of land and progeny and threat of possible removal of a family member important for the continuation of blessing. No wonder its language evokes these two scenes. The author of Genesis 26 is strongly interested in echoing traditions and in making a place for Isaac in the tradition, a theologically motivated writer interested first and foremost in issues of covenant.[54]

As in Genesis 20, the ruler is respectful of proper sexual ethics and conscious of the sin of adultery, but it is noteworthy that Abimelech's character is far less developed than is his scrupulous alter ego in Genesis 20 or even the brusque Pharaoh painted in quick strokes in Genesis 12. No character is developed in Genesis 26—all is subordinated to the covenantal frame that is the author's main interest.

The dating of Genesis 26:1–17 is very difficult. Evidence of language and the conscious reuse of earlier traditions begin to lead to a Deuteronomic or post-Deuteronomic date (post–seventh century B.C.) for the narrative in its current form. Such concrete markers may be the best guides. The land promise is the central concern of the tale, but Israelite insecurity about the rights to the land are surely as old as Israel itself. It does seem clear that if one treats verses 1–17 as a single composition in current form, one must look later in the development of the tradition rather than earlier for a date. The strongly theological interests of the tale surely point to an author whose central motivation is religious, which is not necessarily the case with a wife-sister tale such as Genesis 12:1–10, whose author, though certainly religious, is interested in various aspects of and implications of his heroes' plight.

Three tales present themselves, one popular, one courtly-baroque, one anthological-theological, distinct compositions that share motifs at various levels of narration but exhibit great variation at each level. The descriptive structural analysis leads to some hypotheses about context. Conclusions about composition and transmission seem rather negative at first, rejecting loose notions of oral literature that lead Koch to write of an oral Ur-form of a work like Genesis 26:1–17,[55] rejecting Van Seters's suggestion for a relative chronology for the three accounts, which pictures the author of chapter 20 to have before him the account in 12 and the author of 26 to write with one or both written versions available,[56] rejecting finally source theories to account either for composers or redactor-collectors. With what is one left? Unshackled by the documentary hypotheses, old or new versions of them, the tales do say something about composition. There existed in Israel throughout the centuries different sorts of tale-tellers, popular ones adhering to one style of presentation, courtly ones fulfilling another set of expectations in content and taste, and those whose purpose was homiletical, more thoroughly religious, who tell stories in terms of God's covenant with Israel. Stories told in Israelite tradition, shared by all Israelites, become Yahweh tales first and foremost for narrators in the third category. This is to say quite a bit and is perhaps to be honest with ourselves about the limits of knowledge concerning the composition and preservation of Israelite narrative. The very existence of the Yahwist has always been more a feature of scholarly mythology and worldview than a provable reality. School or individual, composer or redactor, tenth-century Davidite, or ninth-century witness of the fissure between Israel and Judah, we have tended to accept the Yahwist's existence as a fixture of a scholarly cosmology. The work of priestly writers, with its obvious liturgical concerns, genealogical lists, and other repeated features of style and content, is more recoverable, though even in the reconstruction of this source complexity and layering are needed.

Variations on the wife-sister motif are included three times in Genesis. In an approach that treats each tale as an entity in context, one must nevertheless comment upon the larger culture that makes all these tales meaningful to Israelites. Whether we claim the ability to name a final preserver, redactor, composer, or not, the Bible exists now and has existed pretty much in its current form for millennia. Why were these tales preserved and appreciated?

Some have explored the place of each of these tales in the current literary and theological patterns that now reflect the inherited whole.[57] Others have examined the synchronic messages that the tales share on a deep level of structure.[58] We have discussed in detail the appeal of the underdog and trickster patterns, yet Genesis 20 barely qualifies as an underdog tale. The image of a wife declared to be a sister and actual or feared marital relations with foreigners are, however, found in all three. These motifs express deep concerns about Israelite identity and have to do ultimately with exogamy and endogamy, with steering the proper course between marriage inside the group and marriage outside the group, with the fear of incest and the fear of foreigners. At issue are maintenance of the group and its culture and the group's relations with the outside world, its horizons, cultural, social, and economic. All three tales raise "us-them" problems, resolving them in different ways. The pose of the tricksters in Genesis 12 is one of fleeting contact and retreat, sustained distrust and marginality. In Genesis 20, "us" meets "them" on an equal footing, the heroes remaining and prospering in the alien world. In Genesis 26, the underdogs are in a position of divinely protected self-containment in the midst of an alien world. Whether in contact with outsiders or fully apart, they are wrapped in the cloak of the covenant. The wife-sister tales ultimately provide models for the ways in which the "us" and the "them," as variously defined, relate to one another in realms of social reality.

Appendix to Chapter 2

In the fall, when everything was ripe, they had, of course, all they wanted to eat. However, winter soon approached and not long after it began, a deep snow fell. The situation of the four now became indeed very difficult. They had nothing to eat and they were getting quite hungry. Then Trickster spoke, "Younger brothers, it is going to be very difficult. However, if we do the thing I am about to suggest, it will be good. So, at least, I think." "All right, if it is indeed something good that our older brother means we certainly will do it, for otherwise some of us will starve to death. What is it that we should do that is good and by which we can get something to eat?" "Listen. There is a village yonder, where they are enjoying great blessings. The chief has a son who is killing many animals. He is not married yet but is thinking of it. Let us go over there. I will disguise myself as a woman and marry him. Thus we can live in peace until spring comes" "Good!" they ejaculated. All were willing and delighted to participate.

Trickster now took an elk's liver and made a vulva from it. Then he took some elk's kidneys and made breasts from them. Finally he put on a woman's dress. In this dress his friends enclosed him very firmly. The dresses he was using were those that the women who had taken him for a racoon had given him. He now stood there transformed into a very pretty woman indeed. Then he let the fox have intercourse with him and make him pregnant, then the jaybird and, finally, the nit. After that he proceeded toward the village.

Now, at the end of the village lived an old woman and she immediately addressed him, saying, "My granddaughter, what is your purpose in travelling around like this? Certainly it is with some object in view that you are travelling!" Then the old woman went outside and shouted, "Ho! Ho! There is someone here who has come to court the chief's son." This, at least, is what the old woman seemed to be saying. Then the chief said to his daughters, "Ho! This clearly is what this woman wants and is the reason for her coming; so, my daughters, go and bring your sister-in-law here." Then they went after her. She

Excerpt from the Winnebago Trickster Cycle published in Paul Radin, *The Trickster*, pp. 22–24.

certainly was a very handsome woman. The chief's son liked her very much. Immediately they prepared dried corn for her and they boiled slit bear-ribs. That was why Trickster was getting married, of course. When this food was ready they put it in a dish, cooled it, and placed it in front of Trickster. He devoured it at once. There she (Trickster) remained.

Not long after Trickster became pregnant. The chief's son was very happy about the fact that he was to become a father. Not long after that Trickster gave birth to a boy. Then again he became pregnant and gave birth to another boy. Finally for the third time he became pregnant and give birth to a third boy.

The last child cried as soon as it was born and nothing could stop it. The crying became very serious and so it was decided to send for an old woman who had the reputation for being able to pacify children. She came, but she, likewise, could not pacify him. Finally the little child cried out and sang:

"If I only could play with a little piece of white cloud!"

They went in search of a shaman, for it was the chief's son who was asking for this and, consequently, no matter what the cost, it had to be obtained. He had asked for a piece of white cloud, and a piece of white cloud, accordingly, they tried to obtain. But how could they obtain a piece of white cloud? All tried very hard and, finally, they made it snow. Then, when the snow was quite deep, they gave him a piece of snow to play with and he stopped crying.

After a while he again cried out and sang:

"If I could only play with a piece of blue sky!"

Then they tried to obtain a piece of blue sky for him. Very hard they tried, but were not able to obtain any. In the spring of the year, however, they gave him a piece of blue grass and he stopped crying.

After a while he began to cry again. This time he asked for some blue (green) leaves. Then the fourth time he asked for some roasting ears. They gave him green leaves and roasting ears of corn and he stopped crying.

One day later, as they were steaming corn, the chief's wife teased her sister-in-law. She chased her around the pit where they were steaming corn. Finally, the chief's son's wife (Trickster) jumped over the pit and she dropped something very rotten. The people shouted at her, "It is Trickster!" The men were all ashamed, especially the chief's son. The animals who had been with Trickster, the fox, the jaybird and the nit, all of them now ran away.

Trickster also ran away . . .

3. Tales of Two Younger Sons: Contour of the Whole and Style of the Parts

The tales of Jacob and Joseph offer a new set of challenges to the would-be folklorist of biblical literature. Each offers a series of episodes in the lives of these heroes, a cycle of stories that trace a pattern from birth to maturity. The sum of the episodes is biographic on an essential level, a life history,[1] and exhibits qualities of the bildungsroman, the tale of maturation. Each of these lads through his life experiences grows in sensitivity to others and in knowledge of self.[2] Joseph and Jacob are underdogs, youngest sons who inherit, exiles who outwit their masters, marginal people who end their tales with financial and social success.

A first challenge is how to describe the narrative patterns of tales of Jacob and Joseph. Attention to the multilayered quality of elements of narrative content remains important, as does the search for repeated patterns. As in chapter 2, we will be eclectic, experimenting with various approaches to motifs and their combinations.

A second and more basic problem is deciding where each cycle ends. Is it correct to write of separate works, the Jacob cycle and the Joseph cycle? The biographies do intertwine. Within the Jacob cycle is Joseph's birth, a magically induced event belonging to the tale of rivalry between Rachel and Leah. Jacob's father role and his senescence create an important thread of the Joseph cycle as the father loses and then regains his dearest child. On some level, the tales of father and son are part of one composition, and although careful analysis of style, content, structure, theme, and worldview leads to suggestions about different authors and audiences for the two biographies, one level of analysis demands an examination of the whole, of the ways in which the two biographies interact as a composition.

The Pattern of the Hero

Biography, bildungsroman, underdog tale—hero narrative: The hero tale has been the subject of numerous comparativist, synchronic studies (see chapter 1).[3] Such studies draw together a large sample of hero tales and chart out the content shared by them. Working with much of the same material—for example, tales of the lives of Oedipus, Perseus, Hercules, Romulus, Karna, Cyrus, and Siegfried—scholars each produce a set of elements remarkably similar to that of their colleagues, though each has his own interest in tracing the hero tale. Lord Raglan, for example, takes a strongly antihistoricist position and seeks to show that one cannot derive history from typologically and predictably patterned pieces of lore such as the tales of Arthur or Robin Hood.[4] Moreover, he sees the origin of this hero pattern in ritual drama. Otto Rank's psychoanalytical approach treats the hero pattern as the human attempt to grapple with fundamental changes, challenges to our own becoming, central among these being the resolution of relationships with our parents. The hero myth for Rank reflects the conflicting emotions of hostility and gratitude that the child feels for both parents and the need to establish independence apart from them.[5] Rank shares Freud's emphasis on the Oedipus complex but with nuances.[6] Modern folklorists concerned with precise definitions of terms like *myth*[7] or those interested in more closely describing the building blocks of traditional narrative as "functions," "emic," "etic," "actants," and so on would no doubt wince at Raglan and Rank's loose treatment of such matters. They would wish to challenge aspects of Rank's Freudianism and to reject the monolithic, ritual-origins theory of Raglan. Equally objectionable would be Joseph Campbell's abstract monomyth, his suggestion that humans of all cultures think alike,[8] and his all-too-faint lip service to the socioreligious function of myth. Nevertheless, the comparative work on hero patterns indicates that a large cross section of humanity shares an essential story and with it a way of seeing, understanding, and organizing reality. The hero pattern is shared with interesting nuances by the Israelite composers of the Jacob-Joseph tale.[9]

Alan Dundes provides a table comparing the patterns found in the close textual studies by von Hahn, Rank, and Raglan.[10] My annotations indicate a number of motifs shared with the Jacob and Joseph stories (see Table 1).

The motif lists are, as Dundes notes, rather difficult to compare, for each author describes content on a somewhat different "plane of expression." Rank lists as a step in his pattern "hero grows up"; von Hahn describes this step in more specific terms as "hero seeks service abroad." To allow for a better comparison with Jacob and Joseph we can, however, abstract from these lists to a mode of description that will describe all the tales equally well, a common denominator.

1. Unusual birth
2. Family rivalry: conflict over status
3. Journey/adventures
4. Successes in new environment, often including marriage
5. Resolution of rivalry/reunion

Albert Lord suggests an even more inclusive pattern for the traditional tale of the hero, one that strongly emphasizes "key transitional points of life": birth, precocious childhood, transition to maturity, marriage, deeds, death.[11] This mode of expressing the pattern works equally well for all the tales, including those of Jacob and Joseph. The importance of these passage points in each of our lives and their strong presence

Table 1

Von Hahn (1876)	Rank (1909)	Raglan (1934)
1. Hero of illegitimate birth	Child of distinguished parents O△	Mother is royal virgin
2. Mother is a princess	Father is a king	Father is a king
3. Father is a god	Difficulty in conception O△	Father related to mother O△
4. Prophecy of ascendance O△	Prophecy warning against birth (e.g., parricide)	Unusual conception O△
5. Hero abandoned O	Hero surrendered to the water in a box	Hero reputed to be son of god
6. Suckled by animals	Saved by animals or lowly people	Attempt (usually by father) to kill hero O△
7. Hero raised by childless shepherd couple	Suckled by female animal or humble woman	Hero spirited away
8. Hero is high-spirited O△	———	Reared by foster parents in a far country
9. He seeks service abroad O△	Hero grows up O△	No details of childhood
10. Triumphant homecoming △	Hero finds distinguished parents	Goes to future kingdom
11. Slays original persecutors and sets mother free	Hero takes revenge on his father	Is victor over king, giant dragon or wild beast
12. Founds cities △	Acknowledged by people O△	Marries a princess (often daughter of predecessor) O
13. Extraordinary death	Achieves rank and honors O△	Becomes king

Table 1 *continued*

Von Hahn (1876)	Rank (1909)	Raglan (1934)
14. Reviled because of incest and dies young	———	For a time he reigns uneventfully
15. Hero dies as an act of revenge by an insulted servant	———	He prescribes laws
16. He murders his younger brother	———	Later, he loses favor with gods or his subjects
17. ———	———	Driven from throne and city
18. ———	———	Meets with mysterious death
19. ———	———	Often at the top of a hill
20. ———	———	His children, if any, do not succeed him
21. ———	———	His body is not buried, but nevertheless
22. ———	———	He has one or more holy sepulchers

Key to Table 1
$\bigcirc$ = Characteristics common to Joseph
$\triangle$ = Characteristics common to Jacob
$\bigcirc\triangle$ = Characteristics common to both

in traditional hero tales leads Raglan and Lord to write of relationships between such tales and rituals marking passages in the cosmos and in ourselves. Campbell too considers the rite of passage, with its steps of separation/initiation/return, central to the understanding of the hero pattern, though he looks to psychic rather than ritual passages.[12] These approaches, in fact, are not mutually exclusive in the search to understand the prevalence of the hero pattern in the world and its specific use by Israelite authors in the tales of the patriarchs. Lord points to the stages in the actual workaday history of each of our lives; they are mirrored in the psychic process of maturation that accompanies, however harmoniously or inharmoniously, our biological growth. These stages and often difficult passages are recreated, celebrated, and accepted in ritual passages, our own transitions paralleling those we see in nature. They are reflected in our literary patterns—all is of a piece. Table 2 indicates some of the ways in which tales of Jacob and Joseph fulfill the common denominator outline. Campbell would no doubt view the journey as the "separation" step of a rite of passage. Lord's list would have "birth" equal "unusual birth," "conflict" equal "precocious childhood"; Jacob is thus the clever stealer of birthrights, Joseph the dreamer who foretells the future. The journey would be Lord's "transition," his "marriage and deeds" my "adventures abroad," the "death" an ultimate "resolution" following the mature hero's making peace with the world. The broad outline of the hero pattern in Jacob and Joseph narratives leads to two interesting discoveries: first, the pattern is repeated in the lives of father and son; and second, if one adopts a dual layering approach (Bynum's generic vs. nominal) and looks beneath the common denominator motif "resolution," one finds important differences in the specific ways in which this motif is expressed in the Jacob-Joseph narrative versus many of the other traditional-style works.

Family Continuity

A quick look at Dundes's chart (Table 1) indicates that more often than not the hero kills his father or brother in a final resolution of questions about his status in the family, deciding the rivalry in an absolute way. Rank would suggest that such hero "myths" allow one psychically to eliminate the father or father substitute who is a rival for the love of the mother. The pattern provides a sort of wish fulfillment, a safe outlet for

Table 2

Lord	Campbell	Niditch	Jacob	Joseph
Birth		Unusual birth	Barren mother; prayer to and response by divine helper; twin	Barren mother; mandrake magic
Precocious childhood		Conflict: status in family	Jacob vs. Esau; favorite of mother	Joseph vs. his brothers; favorite of father
Transition	Separation	Journey	Flight from Esau; theophanies	Capture by brothers and selling
Marriage/ deeds	Initiation	Adventures abroad; eventual successes	Wives; gaining goods; conflict with Laban/ rivalry	Dream interpretation to become vizier
Death	Return	Resolution	Reconciliation with Esau and return home	Reunion with father and brothers and reconciliation with brothers

deep-seated hostility. The biblical composers deny themselves the outlet; conflict in the Israelite family ends in peacemaking and harmony, this in contrast to the more traditionally typical story of Cain and Abel, an account of rivalry between brothers in antediluvian history. Whereas killing a family member is important to the world-ordering pattern found in tales of Cain and Abel, the *Enuma elish*, Hesiod's *Theogony*, and the tales of Romulus and Remus, it is rejected as a mode of order making here.[13] The peaceful specification of the resolution motif creates an image of unity, wholeness, and cohesiveness among those with close blood ties. The links, though threatened, are restored and strengthened between rival members of the same generation. It is worth emphasizing that viewing motifs in terms of layering—from the general to the more specific—sets in bold relief the Israelite version of the hero tradition, making one more strongly aware of Israelite authors' special messages and concerns. A step in a traditional pattern is specified to emphasize peace rather than further turmoil, reconciliation rather than vengeance, forgiveness rather than a fight to the death.

The presence of the same chain of content in the lives of Jacob and Jospeh furthers the image of wholeness, continuity, and unity of family. The links are thus not only within a generation but between them. The repetition of the same essential pattern of content in one narrative, a trait that Lord and Bynum call "multiformity,"[14] is characteristic of traditional narrative. Such repetition creates literary unity. In the Jacob-Joseph narrative multiformity further weaves together the two biographies to become, on one level, a single composition. The application of the father's story to that of the son is, in fact, one variety of multiformity that the Jacob-Joseph narrative taken as a whole shares with other traditional works. David E. Bynum has shown how the pattern of content in the story of Odysseus' return echoes the tale of Telemachus' journeys from Ithaca to Pylos and from Pylos to Sparta.[15]

Superficially, Homer made the transition from the story of the initiatory hero Telemachus to the story of his father's return by substituting the name of the older hero in the same string of themes he had just used to tell of the son. Such a pattern of multiformity is familiar in oral narrative composition, and in these cases there is usually a logical association which makes it reasonable that the two heroes play the same roles in successive multiforms of the same themes. In the Odyssey, there is a deep connection between the father and his son which made them doubles of each other and required them to share the same patterns of experience.

Bynum suggests that in the Odyssey father-son patterns emphasize the message of "restoration of due authority."[16] In Genesis 25:21–50:26 the repeated pattern emphasizes the succeeding of the younger son, the setbacks and eventual victory of the underdog. Folklore intertwines with theology once God plays the role of helper, as the sureness of God's choice traces the traditional and even predictable pattern of the triumph of the least likely to succeed. Both of these, the typological pattern and the covenantal selection, challenge the ordinary expectations of the establishment, with its rules of primogeniture and inheritance.

The appeal of this pattern is understandable in any period of Israelite history. The messages of wholeness, continuity, and ultimate victory emerging in the repetition of the hero pattern and in the special conciliatory quality of the resolution motif would have been especially uplifting in times of external threat or internal civil war, though a certain national and ethnic insecurity is implicit in Israel's very foundation myths, a part of Israelite ethos and not datable to one particular moment in its history. The hero pattern in its father-son multiformity does establish the Jacob-Joseph tale as a working whole, at least on one broad level of analysis. An author, responding to the patterns of tradition, presents the son in terms of the father, the two of them as traditional heroes. The political and historical implications of this patterned wholeness are great for our view of the final composer who shaped the material in this way. Jacob is Israel, father of all; Joseph is closely identified with the northern tribes, Ephraim and Manasseh. It is, of course, for this reason that one might view the Joseph biography as the only sustained northern composition in the Bible, which we presume to have been edited by southerners. The recurrence of the underdog pattern in the heart of Genesis leads surely to Joseph. He is the next generation's Jacob, the successful younger son whose youngest son in turn will carry on his leadership. The Joseph tale is not an isolated work but through traditional patterning fully integrated into a larger tale of generations. As Telemachus is to Odysseus, so Joseph is to Jacob.

A southern Judaean writer certainly could be responsible for this message, but for such a Judaean, Davidic kingship and/or messiahship, that is, leadership in the line of Judah, is not an important issue. What is important is the overriding message about the victory of underdogs, the wholeness of the people Israel, and the presence of the divine helper involved in the lives of individuals and the community.

Conclusions from an Examination of the Hero Pattern

In tracing the traditional hero pattern one takes account of the Jacob-Joseph narrative, the whole, a work that exhibits this traditional pattern in its father-son multiformity. Themes of unity, continuity, and victory of the younger son emerge in the doubly repeated narrative chain. The resolution motif as specified reveals an important nuance in biblical usage emphasizing the theme of peace within the family. Concerns with unity and reconciliation are not easily datable to one period, but hold meaningful messages throughout Israelite history.

The Jacob-Joseph narrative exhibits some of the primary traits of traditional literature, internal repetition of a narrative pattern that itself is found in an external, cross-cultural range of traditional literature. In its flexibility, the pattern, once suited to a specific culture, reflects and responds to a particular ethos with unique nuances. Having explored the thematic and structural basis for the Jacob-Joseph narrative, comparing the cross-cultural pattern and two Israelite versions, the next step is to take the whole apart. Can one move behind the Jacob-Joseph narrative and juxtapose the biographies of Jacob and Joseph to reveal contrasting works, each of which exists in its own right apart from the whole? This second level of composition criticism distinguishes the tale of Jacob from that of Joseph even while acknowledging their continuous interconnectedness.

Comparison in Style

Style is the important first indicator of the sort of materials with which we are dealing. Scholars have long contrasted the style of the Jacob story with that of the Joseph story, the classic work being that of Hermann Gunkel.[17] Gunkel finds much to compare between Jacob and Joseph stories, each exemplifying the ways in which the storyteller combines and relates individual episodes to create a quite lengthy and unified composition.[18] Yet, like Donald Redford, Gunkel suggests that the Jacob narrative is less unified than the Joseph narrative,[19] a work in which scenes interlock artfully one with the next. With his evolutionary approach, Gunkel regards more episodic works to be more primitive examples of storytellers' art, more integrated works reflecting later, more "modern" tastes and aesthetics. Similarly, though Gunkel finds in both Jacob and Joseph stories the traits of "popular narrative," the "Olrik's laws" of economy in detail, unity of plot, and so on,[20] he views the Joseph narrative as a later form.[21] The Joseph story is discursive, with "an abundance of long speeches, of soliloquies, of detailed descriptions of situations, of expositions of the thoughts of the personages."

The narrator is fond of repeating in the form of a speech what he has already told. Very evidently we have to do here with a distinct art of story-telling, the development of a new taste. This new art is not satisfied, like its predecessor, with telling the legend in the briefest possible way and with suppressing so far as possible all incidental details; but it aims to make the legend richer and to develop its beauties even when they are quite incidental. It endeavors to keep situations that are felt to be attractive and interesting before the eye of the hearers as long as possible. . . .

It is also a favorite device to put substance into the speeches by having what has already been reported repeated by one of the personages of the story (xliii.13, 21, 30 ff.; xliii.3, 7, 20 f.; xliv.19 ff). The rule of style in such repetition of speech is, contrary to the method of Homer, to vary them somewhat the second time. This preference for longer speeches, is, as we clearly perceive, a secondary phenomenon in Hebrew style, the mark of a later period.[22]

Gunkel's tastes are not for this style grown "effeminate," "sentimental," less powerful,[23] aesthetically more sophisticated though it may be.[24] The elaborative sort of repetition, which he contrasts with that of Homer, risks becoming tedious.[25] Especially interesting for our purposes are the stylistic parallels Gunkel draws between the Joseph material and Genesis 20.

Redford's description of the style of the Joseph narrative, or more correctly of what he considers its original version, is much like that of Gunkel, though he makes a different judgment about its aesthetic quality. For Redford, the Joseph narrative in its Reuben version is a fine short story, unified by literary motifs such as the dream, shaped by a sensitive use of irony, its pace controlled and slowed via repetiiton and recapitulation.[26] Redford appreciates its artistry and sophistication and contrasts it with what he considers the more primitive and choppy style of the Jacob-Easu-Laban materials. Redford's study is a complex one, its strengths and weaknesses from the folklorist's point of view already discussed in chapter 1. Style is, for Redford, an important means, not merely of distinguishing the Joseph tale from the Jacob tale, but of weeding out an original Joseph tale that he considers to be tight, sparse, and neat. Later additions to the work exhibit unnecessary and illogical embellishment.[27] The later so-called Judah version based on the earliest Reuben version, a rewrite of it, tends to be wordier, obvious, and redundant. A still later addition in chapter 39 has a tedious, didactic style. Like all source critics, Redford relies on seeming contradictions or doublets in the text to give indication of different contributors in the tradition. Redford wisely rejects the notion that any doublet or seeming contradiction immediately or necessarily indicates the presence of two once independent sources or the work of the redactor. Yet one feels too strongly the hands of Redford the composer, the judge of what makes for a good story, and not strongly enough the approach of Redford the composition critic or Redford the folklorist. When Redford believes material in the Joseph story to be appropriate to the Reuben source, seeming discrepancies in the tale are explained by the psychology of hero or the like. Joseph's self-contradiction in 42:15–16 and 42:19–20 concerning the number of brothers who may return to Canaan does not evidence sources but is appropriate to Joseph's state of mind and witness to "the writer's close observation of his characters."[28] Joseph first reacts in primitive anger, then changes his mind once he calms down. Other repetitions in the tale are, however, evidence of two sources: Judah and Reuben's attempts to keep the lad from being killed (37:26–27 [Judah's] vs. 37:22 [Reuben's]); the scene in which Joseph's brothers explain who they are (42:11, 13) versus the brothers' report of this encounter of their father (43:7).[29] Moreover, Redford's exceedingly detailed study of style in the Joseph story, though careful and erudite, is a bit of a dead end. Redford explores the word order of every clause in the work minus material that he considers to be independent of the plot of Joseph's life, examines various lexicographical aspects of the work, and comes to the conclusion that only chapter 39 stands out from the whole.[30] The three examples of a particular syntactical pattern (object-subject-verb-complement) that set chapter 39 apart for Redford account for only 5 percent of total syntax in that chapter and are not statistically very convincing. Redford's study points to the remarkable homogeneity of linguistic usage in disparate parts of the Joseph narrative, a fact supportive of his case against old-fashioned source theories but unsupportive of his own new-fangled theories about Reuben and Judah versions.

In any event, the technique of stylistic analysis found in Redford's first chapter does not appear to bear much fruit and is not an avenue worth pursuing in comparing and contrasting an even larger slice of the tradition, the lives of Jacob and Joseph. Rather, we will take soundings for the sorts of stylistic criteria explored in our study of the wife-sister tales: (1) brevity of self-contained phrases, (2) the presence of repetition and the varieties of repetition found (e.g., single words, epithets, lengthy passages, exact repetitions, repetition of formula patterns), and (3) length of speeches. In fact, Redford takes some of these soundings in establishing his versions but reaches some wrong conclusions about them. How traditional in style are the Jacob and Joseph narratives? Do the styles of the two contrast sharply according to these criteria, as Gunkel and so many others have asserted? Does one notice striking internal differences in style within each work, as Redford claims to find in the Joseph narrative, with his Reuben version, Judah version, later additions, and general editor?

Brevity of Phrasing

Soundings in the Jacob narrative lead one to appreciate its quality of phrasing, the brief, often disenjambed pieces of information that self-contain and then unfold. The opening two verses of Genesis 27, the deceiving of Isaac, provide a beautiful example of this style—Hemingwayesque in its simplicity, three or four words to a phrase, at times parallel in cadence and meaning. Isaac is old, his age manifested in his blindness. He calls to Esau, his eldest son, and says to him, "My son," and he says to him, "Here I am." And he says, "Behold I have grown old, I know not when I will die." In this case, the self-contained phrases are full clauses, the thought complete at the end of each line; the syntax is repeated, *w*-conversives mesmorizing until the final phrase, "I know not when I will die." Old age parallels blindness in verse 1, death in verse 2. The call and the response "Here I am" echo the terse idiom beginning scores of biblical encounters.

The clarity of phrasing combined with the balance of prose parallelism finds another beautiful example in the tale of the selling of Esau's birthright, Genesis 25:27:[31]

And the boys grew up
Esau became a skilled hunter, a man of the open country,
and Jacob became an acculturated man, dwelling in tents.
Isaac loved Esau because he was game in his mouth,
but Rebecca loved Jacob.

Here three segments have explanatory glosses, all parallel: Esau, a man of the open country; Jacob, a dweller; Esau, game. Thought segments build, as in 27:1–2, to a key phrase, "but Rebecca loved Jacob."

This aspect of style in its varieties has been explored in depth.[32] It is a quintessential biblical narrative style, which influenced Hemingway and others. Does it emerge with less regularity or in a significantly more baroque form in the Joseph narrative? The answer is simply that the same style also predominates in the Joseph narrative and is found, as Redford's more detailed stylistic study indicates, in the seeming doublets of the old-fashioned source critics and in Redford's Judah and Reuben versions.[33] Judah's speech to his father is wordier than Reuben's, but the wordiness is made up of more of the same sort of phrasing. Compare, for example, 42:37 and 43:8–10:

> And Reuben said to his father,
> "Kill my two sons
> if I do not bring him back to you.
> Put him in my hand
> and I will return him to you."
>
> 42:37

> And Judah said to Israel his father,
> "Send the lad with me
> and we'll rise and go.
> We will live and not die,
> we, you, and our children.
> I so pledge.
> From my hand you may exact the penalty.
> If I do not bring him back to you
> and set him before you
> then I have sinned against you for
>   all time.
>
> 43:8–10

Some particularly beautiful examples of this brief, powerful style come at climactic moments of revelation in the tale. When Reuben returns to the pit to find Joseph gone, the text reads:

> And Reuben returned to the pit
> but behold Joseph was not in the pit.
> He tore his clothing.
> He returned to his brothers

and said, "The lad is not there
and I, where shall I go?"

37:29–30

See also Joseph's self-revelation and his brothers' reaction at
45:3:

And Joseph said to his brothers,
"I am Joseph.
Is my father still living?"
But his brothers could not answer him
because they were terrified of him.

Repetition

The stylistic feature that most distinguishes Genesis 12 from
20 and 26 is the presence or absence of traditional-style repetition. Traditional-style repetition is found in both Jacob and
Joseph tales. In lengthy works, repetitions in language may occur from chapter to chapter. These repetitions of specific texts
over large stretches of material are more prevalent in the Joseph
narrative than the Jacob narrative, giving it the smoother, more
integrated stylistic quality noticed by Redford, Gunkel, and
others.

The scene of the stealing of Esau's blessing uses repetition
in a beautifully skilled and traditional way. Reverberating epithets and modifiers for the two sons highlight the relationships
and reversals with which the chapter deals. Esau is called *his*
(Isaac's) elder son (27:1). Rebecca hears Isaac's words to "Esau,
his son" (27:5) and reports to "Jacob, *her* son" (27:6). She dresses
"Jacob, her younger son," in disguise, "in the clothes of Esau
her elder son" (27:15), and gives the delicacies to "Jacob, *her*
son" (27:17). The preference of Isaac for Esau and Rebecca for
Jacob echoes throughout the tale, as does the reminder that the
younger son who should not receive the blessing is about to
do so—all through the simple repeated terms by which the two
sons are called. Similarly, Esau is referred to as "Esau, your
brother" in address to Jacob at 27:6, Esau "my brother" at 27:11,
Esau, "his brother" at 27:30, whereas Jacob is called "Jacob,

your brother" at verse 35. "Your brother has come in guile and taken your blessing." This is a tale about brothers and brother-rivalry, about those for whom ties remain in spite of the tension and the trickery.[34]

Repetition and variation on lengthier pieces of text tie the episode together. Isaac's words to Esau are repeated to Jacob by Rebecca with nice traditional-style variation (27:3, 4 and 27:7), in Rebecca's plans for tricking Isaac (27:9), and in her carrying out of the plan (27:14, 17).

The delicacies to be made, the old man's love of them, the blessing that is to be obtained remind one over and over of the means of trickery and the goal. Isaac's words to the disguised Jacob, "Bring [it] to me and I'll eat of my son's game so that my soul might bless you" (27:25), find repetition in Esau's words to his father, "Let my father eat from his son's game so that your soul may bless me" (27:31). Isaac shudders as he realizes that he blessed "her" son, not "his," and the words of game, eating, and blessing echo again (27:33). The initial problem, the plan, the successful carrying out of the plan, and the closing complication—the trick uncovered—move along via repetition of key language.

The old man's attempt to ascertain the identity of this Esau who sounds like Jacob is slowed down and extended via repetition. Isaac asks Jacob/Esau to "come near that I might touch you." Jacob comes near and he touches him (27:21–22). Isaac asks, "Come near and kiss me." Jacob comes near and kisses Isaac (27:26–27). The "come near" verb in the *qal* plays with its *hiphil* form as investigative affection wrestles with the old man's desire for his food: *haggēšāh lî wĕ'ōkĕlāh . . . wayyaggēš lô wayyō'kal;* "Bring [it] to me that I might eat . . . and he brought [it] to him and he ate" (27:25).

Equally traditional-style repetition is found in the Joseph narrative in Genesis 41. I have discussed this scene of dream solution in some detail in another work.[35] The dreams, framed by the same language, are repeated by Pharaoh and partially repeated in Joseph's interpretation of them.

The frame language is shared with the dream report and interpretation in chapter 40 and with the dream reports in chapter 37 (see also Daniel 7 and 8), a set format for such scenes. In Genesis 41, the dream impossible to interpret is laid before the one wise man who is able to make known its meaning. The heart of the dream/dream-interpretation episode is unified and tightened via repetition of language, the difficulty of the dream web doubly or quadruply emphasized to highlight the ease with which it is unraveled by Joseph.

The pattern of events in Genesis 41 is, as I have shown, a common one in folklore, the scene of dream interpretation a favorite specification of the "impossible problem" in Israel.[36] The author of the Joseph narrative employs traditional material in a traditional way to trace the success of the underdog. Genesis 41, a central point in the life of Joseph, halfway between his expulsion by the brothers and his victory over them, provides an instance of continuity between the style of the Jacob narrative and the Joseph narrative. Yet chapter 41 exhibits one subtle indicator of a variety of repetition that in more pronounced forms does set the Joseph tale apart from the Jacob tale.[37]

When Pharaoh reports his dream to Joseph he embellishes the report with a bit of commentary: Such sickly cows Pharaoh has never seen in all of Egypt! Repetition in the Joseph story is often of a special embellishing variety, as Redford has noted. In exploring style one must examine not only whether or not repetition is used—for the Joseph narrative makes full use of repetition both within individual episodes and throughout the life story to unify the whole, to create allusions, and to develop characters—but also what sort of repetition is used. Chapter 41 exhibits a form of repetition comparable to that of Genesis 27, with one example of embellishment, but chapter 39, the story about the rejection of Potiphar's wife, and 47:13 ff., the rendition of the Egyptians' loss of land, properties, and freedom during the famine, evidence full-blown examples of a baroque style of repetition found in various guises throughout the Joseph story.

Genesis 47:13 ff. exhibits an adding style not uncommon in

traditional literature, for example, the "cumulative tales," types 2000–2199 in the Thompson Index or the Mesopotamian account of the descent of Ishtar to the nether world (*ANET* 106–109). This sort of repeated frame with a heightening of stakes or increasing of number is, in fact, also found in the account of the plagues in Exodus and is in its own way an effective mode of heightening tension, of capturing the interest of an audience. And so we find the repetition of money being gone (47:15, *wayyitōm*) and then another year (47:18, *wattitōm . . . tam*), the people come to Joseph (*wayyābō'û 'el yôsēp/'ēlâw*) and say (*lē'mōr/wayyō'měrû*, vv. 15, 18), "For what purpose should we die before you?" (*negdekā*, v. 15; *lě'ênêkā*, v. 19).

The money is handed over, then the cattle, then the people themselves and their land. The repetition in language gives an impression of gradual stripping bare; the situation grows worse and worse as one is led through the gradual emptying of possessions, forms of self-identity, and personal independence. The repetition frame of Genesis 47, however, includes interesting variations of language compared to the more homogenous examples from *ANET* and the Thompson Type-Index. Contrast the two ways of saying that all financial resources were depleted in 47:15, 16 and 47:15, 18 ("the money has come to an end"; "the money is finished") and the three ways in which the author refers to transactions between Joseph and the Egyptians in 47:16 and 47:20 ("Let's have your . . . and I'll give . . ."; "and he acquired"; "they sold"). The animal wealth that changes hands is described by a full traditional-style chain only at 47:17 and is abbreviated elsewhere. Thus, though reminiscent of traditional style, Genesis 47:13 ff. also evidences the interest in variation of language that betokens a different sort of literature.

Genesis 39 begins with a dense variety of repetition whereby the same words are repeated and combined, creating some parallelism: verse 2, "he was a successful man"; verse 3, "all that he undertook God made succeed in his hands"; verse 4, "and he appointed him over his house, and all that he had he placed in his hands"; verse 5, "he appointed him over his house and over all that he had" (see also the end of v. 5 and v. 6).

The theme of success grounded in God's blessing is strongly emphasized, albeit, as Gunkel might say, in a somewhat tedious fashion. A similar packing of repetition characterizes the second half of the narrative, effectively providing the unsuccessful seductress a wonderful methinks-she-doth-protest-too-much quality:

And he left his robe in her hand and fled and went outside (39:12)
And when she saw that he had left his robe in her hand and fled outside (39:13)

She, claiming attempted seduction by Joseph, summons the men of the household and reports, "And he left his robe with me and fled and went outside" (39:15). To her husband she repeats the story. This variety of repetition has a building quality, the quality of elaboration to which Donald Redford points, although he considers Genesis 39 to be a case apart from a more restrained mode of elaborative repetition he finds elsewhere in the Joseph narrative.[38] In fact, Genesis 39 is a variation on the same stylistic theme. Note that the narrator's comment on Joseph's complete management of Potiphar's household (39:6) is repeated and extended by Joseph's words to the wife at (39:8–9). Joseph shows himself as ever the upright, even moralistic young man, both proud of himself and loyal to his master at the same time. The elaborative recapitulation is a baroque form of repetition found throughout the Joseph narrative.

The brothers' statement to Joseph explaining their identity and their goals and his demands of them (42:10–20) is echoed at 42:30–34 in a report to Jacob and at 43:3–7 when the brothers remind Jacob of their situation vis-à-vis the Egyptians. In the latter appears a detail not found in the scene at 42:10–20. The crafty old Jacob asks why the brothers were so foolish as to reveal details about themselves (43:6); in response they fabricate a question by Joseph (43:7). In Judah's recapitulation, a plodding, Polonius-like speech to Joseph at 44:18–34, this detail is included as if it had taken place in chapter 42; the conversation with Joseph is repeated, as are the words of Jacob, his request to go for food (43:2), his fears for his sons (42:36, 38), and Judah's reassurances to him (43:9). This elaborative recapitulation reviews the events of the story for the reader, who probably requires a review no more than Joseph does. The speech helps to create the character Judah, long-winded and fearful about the new sin he has brought upon his head (44:32); most important of all, it delays the revelation of Joseph's identity, which comes, as we noted, in contrastingly quick, staccato phrases at 45:3.

Another example of elaborative repetition is found at 42:27 and 43:19 ff.: the money paid for grain is discovered in the sacks; when the brothers return to Egypt they seek to explain the incident employing some of the language of 42:27 and more.[39]

In contrast to lengthy repeated passages in the Homeric epics[40] and the Mesopotamian epics, the *Enuma elish* and *Gilgamesh*, this form of repetition is not economical. Again "economical" does not mean "brief" but rather that same content is conveyed by same language, sometimes by exactly the same language, other times by variations upon the same patterns of language. In the Joseph account, the repetitions are more a matter of repetition with elaboration and paraphrase than traditional-style economy of language. The elaborative repetitions are reminiscent of traditional style and may reflect conscious evocation or imitation of traditional style. This baroque form of repetition serves many of the same functions as traditional repetition, creating unity and emphasis and providing review for audiences, but does not serve its compositional functions.

It may be no coincidence that the recapitulations are found in speeches, Joseph's speech to Potiphar's wife, the brothers' self-defense to their father, the brothers' self-defense to Joseph's aide, and Judah's speech to Joseph. The hero in the Joseph account, or the would-be hero, is the one who talks well, convincingly, diplomatically, eloquently, and often in his own defense. Speech making is one aspect of wisdom employed by rascals and heroes alike in biblical traditions about wise men.[41]

Elaborative Repetition in the Jacob Narrative?

The Jacob narrative displays fine traditional-style repetition in individual episodes. As in any piece of biblical literature, much of its prose falls into well-worn patterns on the difficult-to-define boundary where the idiomatic meets the formulaic. The sorts of repetition we have just explored in the Joseph narrative—the adding frame tempered by variation in language, the intense repetition in a brief space, and especially the elaborative repetition or recapitulation—are not found in the story of Jacob. In a few places an author may be creating linguistic links with previous passages: 29:16, 18, when Leah and Rachel are referred to as *haggĕdōlāh* and *haqqĕtannāh*, "the elder and the younger," may allude to chapter 27 (but contrast 29:26); 30:14, 16, "Give me please from your son's mandrakes, . . . When Jacob came from the field" may echo the cadences of 25:29, 30. If so, however, these are subtle literary allusions, not narrative recapitulations in which previous actions or events are reported or reviewed via reiterations that link long stretches of the story.

The Jacob narrative approaches the elaborative repetitive style in the speech to the wives at 31:10–12. Here Jacob provides a new detail not found in the original account of his staves' magic, much as Joseph's brothers add a detail in their report of the encounter with Joseph. Jacob announces that he had received a dream vision from God alerting him that the spotty goats were to be his. The language here slightly echoes that of chapter 30 (cf. 30:32; 30:39; and 31:10, with variation in the chain of "mottle terms"). Jacob's speech to Laban then echoes only one phrase of the speech to the wives (31:7 and 31:41).

In the hands of the Joseph writer these speeches would have included not only elaboration and paraphrase but extensive recapitulation as well, the baroque form of repetition. So too in Jacob's speech to Esau: this encounter between feuding brothers who have not met for years is remarkably brief, including no review of Jacob's life and adventures or of the brothers' conflicts. The Joseph composer would have lengthened the scene and the speeches with the recapitulation technique.

Conclusions on Style

The Jacob and the Joseph account share certain stylistic traits but are also easily distinguished. Brevity of phrasing characterizes both, as does repetition. Though chapters 41 and 47:13–21 of the Joseph narrative evidence fairly traditional style, with the variations already discussed, repetition for the most part in the Joseph narrative is of a more elaborative baroque variety. Although the Jacob account gives some evidence of elaborative style in chapter 31, its repetition is quite traditional in style and is confined to individual episodes. As we proceed to examine patterning of content in each narrative, I make a suggestion: traditional style is to elaborative repetition as theophanies are to dream accounts, as tricksters are to wise men, and as famous fathers are to famous sons: related, interconnected, yet different.

4. Jacob and Joseph: Patterns and Content, Digging Deeper

Within the repeating tale of father and son lie additional layers of patterning that add to and deepen an understanding of the lives of Jacob and Joseph as literary compositions. Adapting the methodology of chapter 2 to these larger pieces of material, we delve into the special nuances of each of the broadly defined motifs of the hero pattern.

To describe the content of the hero pattern in terms of unusual birth, family conflict involving status, journey, adventures abroad, and resolution is to find essential similarities in a cross-cultural group of tales. What, however, makes for the unusual birth or the journey in one or another tale? What images, scenes, tones and settings, narrator's statements, and dialogues or other modes of interaction between characters create the "unusual birth" or the "journey" in a particular tale and with what effects? What is the significance of a particular rendering of the unusual birth? How does it reflect the meanings of the tale, deep or surface, its symbolic resonances, its messages from an author, the sociological and anthropological realities behind it, and the expectations for story telling that helped to shape it?

At this deeper level of analysis emerge certain cross-culturally shared notions of what may constitute the unusual birth: for example, twinning, barrenness of the mother, predictions about the hero before or at birth. The question then becomes why an Israelite author chooses from the story-telling stock of world tradition a particular mode of expressing unusual birth.

In fact, Israelite authors appear to prefer certain bits of this stock—barrenness of the mother and predictions about the hero being special favorites—and express these bits in particular ways: for example, the annunciation scene for the prediction about the hero.[1] It is at this point that folklore studies intersect with biblical form-criticism. There are, then, certain ways Israelite authors "do" unusual birth. As expected, however, individual Israelite authors find their own places in the tradition and may come from different settings within Israelite culture, courtly versus popular, monarchic period versus non-monarchic period, and so on. If as folklorists we respect authors as individual artists or artisans and if as biblical composition critics we are prepared to think in terms of composers of texts set in time and place, then we must be prepared to look behind the shared forms to see what makes the shared piece of tradition special, fresh, and specific to a particular rendering of a tale. In the process we may learn a great deal about the workings of Israelite literature and further prove the feasibility of writing about a Jacob author and a Joseph author.

Unusual Birth

Jacob

To write of "unusual birth" is already to specify a more generic narrative pattern that recurs over and over not only in the Jacob tale but also in the tales upon which Vladimir Propp based his famous set of functions: problem-or-lack/response/lack-liquidated-or-resolution. This is greatly to simplify Propp's lengthy list, but these steps are surely at the heart of his outline of Russian "wondertales." In the Jacob tale the lack is the lack of children; the response, petition to a helper; the resolution, the conception and birth of a child—in fact, two children.

This typology is a common one in folklore. In the Turkish tale "Husnuguzel,"[2] a patishah and his wife lack a son. A helper, an old man with white hair, tells the patishah that he and his wife should share a special apple that grows on a tree behind their palace. They do so and the wife bears a son. Here the connectives are a helper and magic food. The Jacob narrative reflects the favorite Israelite version of this typology, as noted by A. B. Lord, Ronald Hendel, Michael Fishbane, and others:[3]

Generic Elements	Typological Elements	Israelite Version
Problem	Childlessness	Barrenness of woman
Response	Petition to helper	Prayer to God, annunciation scene
Resolution	Conception and birth	Birth of twins

The cause for the childlessness is the barrenness of the wife—so Sarah, so Rachel, so Hannah, and so Samson's mother. Note that both husband and wife require cures in the Turkish tale. The petition, a simple narrator's line (Gen. 25:21),[4] is followed by an annunciation, a message to the mother about the identity and future of the children to be born (Gen. 25:23). Alter refers to this recurring content cluster as a type-scene.[5] Such scenes of annunciation in Scripture involve both pregnant women such as Hagar and women soon to conceive such as Sarah and Samson's mother. The twinness of the brothers is another common feature of unusual birth in world folklore, here employed by an Israelite author who develops the theme of brother rivalry and preference for the younger. The prebirth image of the twins struggling within Rebecca, also a non-Israelite specific image (Thompson motif T575.1.3), intertwines with the next motif of the narrative pattern, indeed, commences it.[6] In this case the message is that the elder will serve the younger. Folk etymologies for the names of the children further color the unusual birth of the hero, establishing at the outset part of his character and identity. Jacob is "a grabber of heels" (Gen. 25:26).[7] Themes of rivalry and status at the heart of the entire narrative of Jacob as trickster are textured into the very opening of the hero's life. Brother rivalry and the younger's attempts at usurpation are implicit or explicit in the occasion for the annunciation, the annunciation itself, the very doubleness of the birth, and the folk etymology for the name Jacob. It is particularly interesting that in Israel, the wife, not the husband, is always the barren one; the woman is associated with fertility or lack of fertility. The annunciation centering on the birth of her children becomes the major biblical occasion for communication between God and women, in fact, some of the few scenes in which God directly addresses women. Woman is the child bearer, her power a home-oriented, family-centered, sexual power. The future of the great men is conveyed and confirmed through her in the very process of birth and in divine communications received by her before, during, or soon after pregnancy.

The role of woman as container and conveyer of the hero's future continues as Rebecca becomes Jacob's co-trickster, helping to bring to reality the message of the annunciation. The image of container and conveyer, of vessel, is in fact the dominant one of women in Israelite and later classical Jewish literature, with all the potential ambivalences that image reflects and effects.[8]

Joseph

The unusual birth of Joseph is part of the Jacob cycle (Gen. 30:1–24). In Jacob's life it constitutes one of his experiences abroad. The generic pattern, lack/response/resolution, reveals a rather interesting variation on Genesis 24:21 ff. The lack involves children, the cause of infertility again being the barrenness of the wife. The resolution again is the birth. In this case, however, the connective is not petition. This independent Jacob, who actually sets conditions in forming a relationship with God at 28:20–22, does not at this point pray. In fact, instead of the simple barrenness/petition-to-divinity/miraculous-granting in Isaac's story, this episode of unusual birth is expanded by some fiercely realistic detail. Rachel, desperate for children, which are a veritable source of identity for the women of Scripture, the means by which they are integrated into their husband's families,[9] says to Jacob, "Give me children or I will die" (Gen. 30:1). Jacob retorts not with the patience of Elkanah but with fiery sparks of anger, betraying, perhaps, his own disappointment and bitterness (30:2). The lack of children creates tension between the lovers, their marriage so long delayed. Now patience dissolves as husband and wife are marginalized by the barrenness of the favorite wife.[10] "Am I in the place of God who has withheld from you the fruit of the womb?" (30:2). Implicit is the message, "This is your fault, not mine. This is between you and God." Here the burden of women as conveyer/container emerges. Could Jacob's retort mask his own fears that the childlessness of his favorite wife is somehow related to his shabby treatment of Isaac and Esau?

In any event, the interaction between Jacob and Rachel further emphasizes that the lack of children is an issue of status: for the woman, her proper fulfilled status as child bearer in the patriarchal clan, for the man, his place in the generations of his relatives. Jacob wishes his place to be continued not by a concubine's son or by the sons of Leah, the wife of trickery, but by the child of his beloved, the rightful wife of his choice. One can fill out the generic elements, "problem" and "resolution" at a specific level, "marginal status" and "status corrected." At the typological level we find "childlessness" and "birth." The connector between the two elements at the typological level is magic, specifically a fertility plant, the mandrake. The narrative in chapter 30, in fact, has two connectives, God's remembering Rachel at verse 22 and the mandrakes. As in the staves incident (30:37–43), the biblical writer is a bit uncomfortable in leaving magic as magic. Thus we find Jacob performing sympathetic magic to produce animals of a certain stripe and later his report of a dream in which God shows himself aware of and in control of the sorts of flocks that are born (31:10–13). So too here the efficacy of mandrakes is aided by divine action. The two links to the birth of Joseph do not stand in absolute contradiction. Rather in this way the author employs a traditional morphology whereby magic cures a status problem (cf. Cinderella type 510) and a cross-cultural typology whereby a fertility potion cures infertility (e.g., "Husnuguzel"; see Motif Index T511.1.1), with an Israelite nuance that reflects the author's and the audience's particular religious interests. The association of women with the power of the household, the hearth, fertility and sexual matters, the power of the private realm,[11] is nowhere more evident than in the scenes between Rachel and Leah and Jacob and Leah. The women trade conjugal rights for mandrakes, and Leah then informs Jacob that his sexual services have been sold to her like those of a hired prostitute.[12]

Conclusions from Two Births

Much more is said about Jacob's actual birth than about Joseph's, for Joseph's birth is announced by the writer who is more interested in the hero Jacob; hence the annunciation and so on in Jacob's birth story. The story of Joseph's birth serves to contrast Jacob and Isaac more than Jacob and Joseph. In contrast to Isaac, Jacob does not turn to God at this point. He and his wife, moreover, are portrayed in a psychologically realistic and powerful way. Rachel's barrenness provides the unusual birth for Joseph, of course, but predictions about his future and insight into his character await the work of another author and another sort of literature. It is interesting in this context that Joseph's own wife will not be barren, nor will her character be developed. The morphological pattern, problem-in-status/ magic/status-improved, is of course reminiscent of the trickster and underdog patterns of the wife-sister stories, a point to which we will return.

Our study of unusual birth serves to establish a methodology. A description of what constitutes unusual birth event in each narrative reveals variations on a morphological pattern that makes for the hero's birth in each case. Cross-cultural comparisons set the births at morphological and typological levels within a rich fund of folk literature. Special Israelite nuances emerge in the process: the annunciation scene, present in the

Jacob's birth and not in Joseph's; the barrenness of the wife. These nuances in turn lead to reflections upon views of women in Israelite literature. Given that the Joseph birth takes place in the story of Jacob, we find less emphasis on Joseph than on Jacob and fewer expectations for him. Both birth accounts, however, reveal the concern with changing status, a change that may be mediated and effected in various ways. The emphasis on status, lost and gained, is the key to the study of underdog and tricksters.

Brother Rivalry

The brother rivalry is a recurring motif in the Old Testament, found in stories of Cain and Abel, Ishmael and Isaac, Jacob and Esau, and Joseph and his brothers. The scene in which Jacob blesses Ephraim and Menasseh provides faint echoes of the rivalry. It is one variation on the "family conflict" that figures so prominently in creation myths.[13] Otto Rank suggests that the older brother is a father substitute in a more basic patricidal mythic pattern.[14] And indeed we note that in the Jacob tale both Isaac and Esau are duped. Joseph's dreams in chapter 37 include symbols of the parents bowing down as well as the elder brothers. The preference of a parent for one of the sons is common in folklore.[15] Ronald Hendel and others suggest that the author of the Jacob tale prefers culture over nature, Jacob, the *îš tām* (the acculturated man), over the ruddy and rough Esau.[16] The preference for the younger son has antiestablishment and serendipitous implications, as we noted earlier. In the tales of Jacob and Joseph, the brother rivalry is central to each of the narratives as a whole; each work reaches conclusion only once the tension between brothers is resolved. Events along the way, "journey" and "adventures," serve to highlight the brotherly conflicts, which are central.

Jacob

The Jacob narrative includes two trickster tales about the stealing of Esau's rights of primogeniture. Each, like Jacob's birth, fits the generic pattern of problem/response/resolution. The resolution is not a permanent one. The problem concerns status, the response is trickery, and the resolution increased status, but the trickster, once discovered, must flee. This morphological pattern is shared with the content and structure of Genesis 12:10–20:

Morphology	Typology in Genesis 27
Marginal status	Younger son meant to receive blessing, but his father plans to give it to the elder son
Deception	Disguise: to make father think he is the elder
Improved status	Younger son receives blessing
Deception uncovered	He is found out
Return to outsider status	Flight and a new series of tricks

Rebecca is Jacob's helper, playing a major role in the planning of the ruse as well as in the escape. Rebecca is a virtual co-trickster. As in Genesis 12, God is in the wings as helper and determinator. Note that the father's power is challenged here as well as the elder son's, reminding us of Otto Rank's suggestions about the link between elder brothers and fathers in such tales of usurpation.

Characterizations in chapter 27 offer fine contrast between the fool and the clever trickster. Gunkel contrasts the emotional restraint of the Jacob tale with the Joseph tale's emotional excess. Isaac's great shuddering at 27:33—literally, "and Isaac trembled exceedingly much an enormous trembling"—when he realizes what has happened and Esau's crying out with an exceedingly great and bitter cry at verse 34 and again raising his voice and weeping at verse 38 provide moments as emotional as any scene in the Joseph tale.

As in chapter 25, Jacob, the trickster, shows little emotion at this point; he plots, he schemes, he is cunning. The defeated Esau and the duped old man are the ones without control.

Isaac, Esau, and Jacob thus provide biblical examples of the wise and the foolish, and God's sympathies are with the wise, or perhaps we should say the wily.

Not all scholars would recognize the scene in 25:29–34 as a trickster episode. The interpretation depends on the understanding of verses 31–33. Does this scene portray an honest deal—pottage for a birthright—or extortion by a clever con artist, Jacob—a ravenous and foolish man is offered food for something much more valuable? The trade that puts the fool at disadvantage is a common scene in folklore. (See Motif Index K134.4–139.1; 149.1 for tricksters' unfair exchanges.) The mistake of the duped Esau is to assume that real food here and now is better than some abstract notion of birthright for which the rewards are distant. The careful planner, Jacob, again contrasts with the fool, who lives for the moment. Ronald Hendel's suggestions about preferences in the tale for culture over nature come to mind.[17] Genesis 25:29–34 thus provides an initial and incomplete working out of the trickster pattern fully articulated in chapter 27.

Joseph

In the Joseph account, no trick allows the younger to inherit, nor does a prebirth annunciation predict Joseph's success. The prediction and the confirmation of his success come within his own symbolic dreams in a form of wisdom that differs from trickery. The symbolism of Joseph's dreams (Genesis 37) is transparent to all but the young Cassandra-like Joseph, who naively reports the dreams to his brothers, already made jealous by the coat gift, evidence of their father's preference, and already outraged by Joseph's special intimacy with his father, evidenced by Joseph's reporting to Jacob about their presumed indiscretions. Some would see in Joseph an upstart, a tattletale, a papa's boy, and one who consciously insults his brothers with his dream reports. The upstart then matures, growing in self-understanding and wisdom. This is to misread the characterization. Joseph matures in the sense that he learns to use his

God-given wisdom and his abilities, but his character is quite consistent throughout the tale. The dreadfully honest lad who reports to his father about his brothers and who recounts his dreams so accurately grows up to be as loyal to Potiphar as to Jacob and as ethically self-righteous as in his youth, refusing the advances of his lord's wife. His later treatment of his brothers does not exemplify petty vengeance, as Redford implies,[18] but is the perfect enactment of just deserts. The mention of Jacob's love for Joseph, the robe, and the two dream reports immediately establish Joseph's status as the child to inherit. As Joseph later tells Pharaoh in wisdom characteristic of the lore of ancient Near Eastern dream interpretation, the doubly dreamt dream is especially reliable, its doubly sent message confirmed and true.[19] The remainder of the Joseph tale works out the fulfillment of Joseph's own prediction about himself. He himself is a conduit of God's word; his future is set not in his mother's divine communication but in his own.

And yet at this early point in the narrative, the tale is not told from Joseph's point of view, but from the vantage point of the jealous brothers. It is their status that is in question, threatened by the God-sent dreams and their father's overt preference. In the Jacob tale, the father's preference is for the elder, as it should be; it is not at all clear that Jacob will inherit. The hero thus in antiestablishment fashion, aided by a woman, responds with trickery. In the Joseph tale, father and Joseph appear to be conspiring to give the youngest rights of primogeniture, and so, seeing Joseph coming, the brothers hastily conceive a plan and temporarily resolve their problem. The resolution of their problem, of course, sets into motion the heart of Joseph's story. The morphological pattern that describes this part of the story from the brothers' point of view is strikingly similar to the trickster/underdog pattern we have seen before:

Question of proper status, marginality
Treachery, a form of cleverness/deception
Status clarified

At this level we begin to see a plane on which meet deception, trickery, cleverness, magic, wisdom, and treachery. A question of status is addressed by manipulative activity of some kind. Variations on this morphology characterize both the Jacob and Joseph tales. And yet the brothers are not successful tricksters. They will be thoroughly defeated and supplanted at the end of the tale. Indeed, in contrast to the Jacob tale, the Joseph tale is not protrickster or antiestablishment. This is why the characterization of Joseph as honest, aboveboard, and ethical must be consistent throughout.[20]

At the typological level this portion of the Joseph tale shares content and pattern with portions of other traditional literature. For example, in the Turkish tale "The Blind Padishah with Three Sons," collected in August 1964 from Sukru Daryi, a custodian working in Davshit, Chorum, Turkey,[21] a youngest son returns from a successful quest, having been the only one of three brothers able to find the magic cure for his father's blindness; his brothers, jealous of his new status, dig a deep well at the crossroads and trap him within it. They tell their father that wolves have killed him, presenting their father a bloody shirt as evidence. The lad goes on to survive, have adventures, and return home and kill the brothers, taking his rightful place beside his father. A particular specification of the morphology questionable-status/treachery/temporary-firm-status in a tale of brother rivalry is thus shared cross-culturally. Elsewhere we have explored the motif of rivalry in the family as an expression of human maturation and self-individualization. It is a way in which the primeval world of gods is often imagined to become and unfold. Images of crossroads and stays in wells or pits are equally universal markers of transition in traditional narrative. The hero, a passenger in his odyssey, has adventures at a boundary. He is made a temporary nonperson, dead or thought dead or naked, below the earth. His old persona, his youth or former status, is undone and stripped bare so that he can change and emerge as someone else, older, with new status and responsibility.[22] With his emergence from the pit and subsequent adventures, Joseph, like the hero of the Turkish tale, commences a transformation.

Journey

Jacob and Joseph

What is drawn out and what is abbreviated in a tale is important. The journey from the land to Egypt receives less than a line in the Joseph tale ("They brought Joseph to Egypt," 37:28). The travels of Jacob, however, contain a powerful incident, an encounter with God. In the narrative pattern of the Jacob tale the theophany is an Israelite expression of the acquisition of a helper. This scene of acquiring a helper is rich in symbolic resonances of rites of passage shared across cultures.

The dream experience on the road to Haran, like Joseph's descent into the pit, is a marker of passages. Jacob, his mother's favorite, leaves home and childhood behind to acquire his own wife and children.[23] The classical discussion linking visions of ladders, *axis mundi*, and initiation experiences is that of Mircea Eliade.[24] Like the Eskimo shaman or Manchu holy man, Jacob peers through a window into the divine realm and sees God. God identifies himself formulaically, reiterates the promise to the fathers, echoing words to Abraham (see my work on Genesis 26 in chapter 2). In folkloric terms, Jacob, like so many underdogs on the road to success, acquires a helper who will further his goals. In Israelite terms, the acquisition of a helper is a scene of covenant making, with its identification of God (28:13), its land promise (28:13), its promise of progeny (28:14) framed by the dream theophany, an Israelite medium of divine communication. Thus, the journey, one step in the life of the hero with obvious and literal transition-making significance, comes alive as the hero is shown momentarily through a dream to cross the boundary between heaven and earth. This crossing articulated by an Israelite author for Israelite audiences has the familiar markings of the theophany/covenant. The helper who reveals himself to the crosser of boundaries is in the Israelite scene Yahweh, God of the fathers, creator and transformer.

The naming of the place "House of God" (28:19) underscores the significance of this dream experience—Jacob has entered another realm and been transformed—and the vow he makes at 28:20–22 further draws the hero's character. "If God will be with me . . ." Jacob sets conditions for his relationship with and loyalty to the divine helper. This response to the theophany is remarkably in character for Jacob, trickster and bargainer. The specifics of his terms to God ("if I return in peace to my father's house . . .") anticipate the return crossing when he will more literally wrestle with God.

In contrast to Jacob, Joseph experiences no theophany. His symbolic and nontheophanic dreams constitute an initiation into favored-by-God status. The dreams revealing the future are also experiences of the otherworldly, God-sent, and mantic but are a less dramatic way of including the divine helper in the tale than Jacob's dream theophany. The differences between the heroes' dreams point, in fact, to a major difference between the tales. God explodes into the Jacob narrative, appearing at significant transitional points and then receding, very much like the helpers of traditional literature, but the God of Joseph is a quieter and more constant presence.[25] The words of the narrator, of Joseph himself, and of Pharaoh allude to God's role in furthering Joseph's success and the success of those around him. (See, for example, 39:2, 21–23; 41:16, 38–39.) God's words are never doubted, even by the non-Israelite Pharaoh. The tale is controlled by God from the outset; its characters recognize that control. Such is the nature of Israelite proverbial wisdom, a wisdom grounded in fear of the Lord that contrasts with the trickery of the Jacob tale even while being related to it.

Successful trickery is also a form of wisdom, requiring forethought, planning, cleverness; it too is an attempt to achieve temporary control of one's environment. But tricksters are more quixotic than wisdom heroes; like humor, trickster narratives rely on surprise to be effective, on doubt. Thus Jacob doubts Yahweh; as a trickster, he must credit God with being as complex and unpredictable as he is. The God of the tale mirrors its hero. The trickster experiences wrestling God-men, whereas the wisdom hero experiences a more steady hand; the trickster sees God face to face, whereas the wisdom hero receives his messages through symbolic dreams. He evidences the God within him through the ability to unravel the meaning of others' dream symbols, the symbolic dream itself being a veiled form of divine communication requiring the skills of mantic wisdom to be understood.[26]

Adventures

Jacob

The major scenes in Haran are (1) the meeting at the well (29:1–12), (2) the incident of the mistaken bride (29:15–30), (3) the rivalry between wives and the mandrakes episode (29:31–30:24), (4) the magic sticks for acquisition of father-in-law's wealth (30:25–43), (5) the preparations for flight and beginnings of resolution (31:1–16).

The adventures of Jacob include the acquisition of a wife, trickery by the father-in-law on the marriage night, the hero's return trickery of his father-in-law, and flight. The rivalry with Esau involving trickery finds echoes in the rivalry between son-in-law and father-in-law (nephew and uncle) at Haran but also in the rivalry between the wives of Jacob.

The acquisition of the wife is, as A. B. Lord notes, a common piece of the hero's adventures abroad, the meeting at the well one of the Israelite authors' favorite expressions of this motif, as noted by Alter and others.[27] Most recently Ronald Hendel has emphasized the fertility symbolism of water and wells.[28] This brief scene is followed by two fine examples of the trickster morphology, the dominant literary pattern of the Jacob narrative. Laban plays trickster in the first, whereas Jacob resumes his trickster role in the second.

Laban's Trickery

Generic	Specific	Typological
Problem	Questionable status	Ugly daughter without suitors
Plan/response	Deception/trickery	She is palmed off as the beautiful daughter
Execution/resolution	Improved status	She becomes a wife and regularized
Complication	Deception uncovered	Her true identity is discovered in the light of day
Reversal	Trickster is tricked	Dupe steals trickster's wealth so that his status increases at trickster's expense

Laban's problem is that his elder daughter is unattractive and undesirable. She is an outsider, a marginal person for whom her father must take responsibility until he can marry her off and regularize her position. Old maids are anomalies in Israel along with widows and unmarried nonvirgins.[29] The parallel with other sorts of marginality is clear. Laban as trickster takes the situation into his own hands. Playing the Rebecca role, he disguises the child as the one desired by the other party, who is unknowingly about to regularize the marginal one's status. The just-deserts quality of this episode has not been missed by scholars over the years. He who cheated an elder out of his birthright is to be cheated by an elder and her father. Ironies in Laban's excuse to Jacob—"It is not the done thing in our area to give the younger in marriage before the elder"—have been duly noted, for placing the younger over the elder contrary to custom is precisely what Jacob and Rebecca do in the case of Esau. The pattern of trickery/trickster-duped/reverse-trickery and plays on older-younger rivalry are ways in which the author ties together the Jacob narrative into a beautifully balanced whole. Not only are there parallels between Genesis 27 and Laban's deception of Jacob; there are also essential parallels between this passage and the stealing of the birthright in chapter 25, if both are seen to involve unfair trades or deals. In this case Laban off-loads the undesirable woman, holding back the desired one to obtain seven more years of work from "the buyer," Jacob. The wife switch is, of course, a common typological motif of the trickster. Recall our discussion of Genesis 12:10–20, in which the wife-sister is a variation on the disguised wife motif. In this way, the stock of traditional taletelling—wife switches, unfair bargains—is transformed by the skillful composer into the stuff of another tale of rivalry and status, essential folk themes at the heart of all underdog tales. One scene of trickery parallels another as the fine balance of the Jacob tale begins to emerge:[30]

A	Brother scene (conflict and trickery)
B	Trickery against father (older vs. younger; disguise)
C	Flight
D	Encounter with God
B	Father-in-law trickery against son-in-law (older vs. younger; disguise)
A	Sister scenes (conflict and rivalry)
B	Trickery against father-in-law
C	Flight
D	Encounter with God
A'	Brother scene (reconciliation)

We have discussed the mandrakes incident in some detail under the birth of Joseph, its traditionality, its special Israelite specification, and the relationship of its story pattern to the underdog and trickster morphologies that dominate tales of Jacob and Joseph.

The staves episode in 30:25–43 presents yet another example of the trickster morphology:

Morphology	Typology in Genesis 30
Marginality/status:	Hero lacks own wealth and family headship; he falls between proper statuses.
Deception/trickery:	Hero strikes a deal with his boss and family elder, making it look as if the hero's end of the deal is a poor one. In actuality, magic assures that the opposite is the case.
Improved status:	The magic works.
Deception/trickery uncovered:	Realization that "less" was "more."
Reversal of status:	Flight.

The hero knows he can use magic, the sympathetic magic of staves marked like the animals he wishes to be born, to turn what should be only small profit, a few animals of rare coloration and marking, into considerable profit. The power of the magic is even more impressive since Laban removes the spotty animals from Jacob's reach.

The scene with the wives in chapter 31 we discussed earlier as an example of limited elaborative style. This dialogue is important to the Jacob tale because it begins the process of reconciliation. The wives join together to support Jacob. He virtually asks them if they are for him or for their father; one senses how marginal his status has been in this lengthy rivalry. Are the women *his* wives or still Laban's children?[31] This scene is evocative of a whole range of family problems. The unloved wife and the beloved wife, so long barren, stand together in relation to their husband. Their tensions with their father are now explicit; implicit are tensions between them and between each of them and their husband. If Oden is correct, this scene is a genuine reflection of tensions in the cross-cousin marriage, so that cousins are spouses and uncles fathers-in-law—a closeness, an interweaving of relationships, that leads to inevitable distance. The wives' declaration of their loyalty to Jacob, their allusion to all their children demarginalizes a whole set of relationships. Jacob, the wives, and the children now constitute a nuclear family, at last unified, together planning their escape.

Jacob's mention of a dream theophany in which God tells him that the striped, spotted, and mottled goats are to be his is interesting. We are not told whether this dream motivated the deal with Laban or whether it reflects God's assurance that the magic will work, as in the case of Moses' rod. In this way, divine control is never doubted; God is made a part of the scene without intruding too heavily upon its trickster pattern. So Yahwistic narrative interests live in harmony with more universal folkloristic ones. Some might write of sources. More interesting are the ways in which Israelite specific forms, such as the theophany, contribute to, blend with, and help to express narrative in the traditional style. In this case, the theophany is kept aside from the folktale plot, though it could have been made a more integrated part (i.e., helper gives magic instrument to hero).

Joseph

Redford considers the tale of Potiphar's wife an appendage, an addition to the Joseph story that adds little. Nevertheless he sensitively notes that it reflects a tale popular in the ancient Near East as opposed to a rote borrowing from the Egyptian "Tale of Two Brothers."[32]

If one is attuned to traditional patterns one finds that the encounter with a seductress higher in status than himself is precisely the sort of adventure encountered by a hero. It is for him a test of his independence and of his loyalty to other relationships, a test failed by Lancelot and experienced also by Odysseus (see Thompson motif T481.4: wife seduces husband's servant). Of special interest in religious biographies, attempted seduction often marks initiation experiences in the lives of saints and shamans.[33] It is a test especially appropriate to the ambience of courtly wisdom found in the Joseph tale. The book of Proverbs, Ahiqar, Sirach, and other wisdom collections make much of the necessity to reject inappropriate women, even hypostasizing wisdom as the good woman, folly as the harlot

(Prov. 1:20–33; 6:20–35; 7:10–27), a point emphasized by von Rad.[34] And so, on many levels the encounter fits the larger pattern of the Joseph tale. The narrative pattern of the incident involving Potiphar's wife also relates beautifully to the story of the selling of Joseph.

As in the brother treachery of chapter 37, the pattern of events, the action, is moved along not by Joseph, protagonist and hero of the larger tale, but by the antagonist. Joseph is a passive character acted upon by the others and by the wife of his overlord.

Generic	*Specific*	*Typological*
Problem	Lack of desired status; contradiction between desired status and proper and actual status	Married nubile woman desires a lad who works for her husband
Plan	Entrapment	Seduction
Complication	Entrapment foiled	Rejection by love-object
Outcome	Remaining in original status	Cover-up

In contrast to the trickster morphology worked out several times in the Jacob narrative, here the plot fails; no initial success precedes the uncovering of the trickery. The tale does not develop into a story of the cuckolded husband. The important connecting step, the plan (entrapment), is not an act of cleverness but one of foolhardiness, exemplifying a lack of wisdom. Like Joseph's brothers, Potiphar's wife is a fool. Like a trickster, Potiphar's wife escapes, perhaps to seduce again, but unlike the trickster, she does not succeed and obtain the desired object. Wisdom themes and wisdom-based judgments about characters' actions are implicit throughout the Joseph narrative. We should keep in mind that much of folklore is about the wise and the foolish, as Thompson's motifs J–K indicate (vol. 4 of the Index). The author of the Joseph narrative develops this "folk idea" in accordance with the tenets of ancient Near Eastern wisdom literature; the two intertwine beautifully, or perhaps we should say that in this narrative the two are one.

In this way, the high ethics of the hero Joseph are emphasized. He is the same innocent person who shares dreams with his family in chapter 37, the same self-righteous person who reports on his brothers. His condition as initiate continues as he moves from the pit to slave status and finally to prison, but even now his eventual fate is never in doubt. Joseph lays the groundwork for an eventual elevation through his ability to interpret dreams.

The scene with Pharaoh's imprisoned servants provides introductory material establishing the credentials of the hero for the big scene in chapter 41. The dreamers report their stories to Joseph, who interprets them, and all predicted by Joseph comes to pass.

The Narrative in Genesis 41 from Two Points of View

Told from Pharaoh's point of view, the tale shares a morphology with the first section of the Turkish tale "The Blind Patishah," another part of which we analyzed earlier. In "The Blind Patishah," the missing object is a cure for blindness. The two elder sons fail in their search, while the youngest succeeds curing his father. I have discussed Genesis 41 in some detail under style in chapter 3 and in my book *The Symbolic Vision*. Israelite authors of Genesis 41 and Daniel 2, 7, and 8 had special interest in the puzzles of symbolic dreams. They specify the conundrum accordingly. Here, as in Genesis 20, the juxtaposition of a dream message to a ruler with an entourage of professionals available to advise on dreams lends the incident the ambience of a Near Eastern court. One notes a few other matters. The comparison with "The Blind Patishah" is a reminder that all complex tales are made up of various incidents, dialogues, and so forth, as are the tales of Jacob and Joseph.

Joseph's Perspective

Generic	*Specific*	*Typological*
Problem	Marginal status	Hero is a prisoner and exile
Response	Cleverness/ performance	Hero can solve unsolvables, can interpret dreams, is wise
Resolution	Increase in status	Hero becomes vizier; clothing and name transformed; marries well

Pharaoh's Perspective

Generic	*Specific*	*Typological*
Problem	Missing item	The unknown meaning of a disturbing conundrum
Response	Search	To find a wise man capable of solving the conundrum
Complication	Search fails	All establishment wise men are incompetent
New plan	Second search	Find the unlikely hero, the person of low status reputed to be capable of solving conundrums
Resolution	Missing item found	Hero solves the problem

In "The Blind Patishah" we have uncovered at least two morphological patterns that shape it. The patterns of tales can be examined, moreover, from various points of view. If one outlines the story from Joseph's perspective, a simple underdog

tale emerges; Joseph's rise is meteoric. The rewards of transformed clothing, changed name, new position, and marriage
mark his renovation as a person. Note too that issues of exogamy and endogamy so important in the Jacob account are simply not an issue here. Joseph is made anew, and reaches a new
stage in his life with new responsibilities and roles.

The opportunity to display his cleverness is not created by
Joseph—this in contrast to Abraham's saying his wife is his
sister or Jacob's acquisition of flocks through magic. Joseph is
brought to the king and acted upon. With his successful performance, he becomes the actor rather than the one acted upon;
he controls subsequent episodes. Until this time, God's presence in the tale is especially strong and constant. Joseph's wisdom is, in fact, not merely a matter of human cleverness or
expertise, for who can fathom the symbolic meaning of dreams,
which are experiences of the numinous? Dreams provide a special form of knowledge and are God-sent, prophetic. Pharaoh
acknowledges this God power (41:39), as does Abimelech in
Genesis 20. Joseph, too, insists that the interpretation does not
come from him (41:16). On the one hand, this insistence furthers the impression of Joseph as upright God-fearer, appropriately modest before the real power; on the other hand it also
points to the special numinous quality of dreams. To interpret
dreams in an Israelite context is not merely an exercise of secular wisdom but evidence of divine inspiration.

And yet the underlying pattern problem-in-status/wisdom-
magic-cleverness-trickery-treachery/change-in-status is one we
have seen over and over again in Jacob and Joseph tales. The
pattern serves to emphasize that Potiphar's wife and Joseph's
brothers lack wisdom and Joseph possesses it. Essential to both
biographies are questions of status and forms of manipulation
affecting status, be the manipulation magic, courtly wisdom,
mantic wisdom, or entrapment; these are all deceptions of various kinds, various forms of "sleight of hand."

How do the various manifestations of this morphology reveal
differences in author-audience interests and in questions of the-

ology, ethics, and views of authority that allow us to speculate about authors and audiences? How do an author's choices in pattern of content tally with style and with what significance? How do tales of Jacob and Joseph differ and not differ? We explore the resolution motif in each narrative and then deal with these questions.

Resolution

Jacob

Reconciliation in the nuclear family is accomplished before the departure from Haran; two more scenes of reconciliation are required for the tale to be complete, one between Laban and Jacob and one between Esau and Jacob. Balancing these is an experience of God parallel to the theophany of chapter 32.

Generic	Specific (morphology)	In this Israelite tale
Problem	Marginal status	Jealousy of in-laws upon whom hero is dependent; ambiguous rights to acquired goods
Plan	Deception/trickery	Stealthy departure with goods and theft of in-laws' gods
Complication	Trickery discovered	Father-in-law catches family in flight but does not find his gods
Outcome	Demarginalization	Complete reconciliation and recognition of rights to wealth

Weaving together the final scene with Laban is one more trick, perpetrated by Rachel without the knowledge of her husband. Rachel steals Laban's household gods.[35] Rachel is never discovered to be the trickster. By telling her father she is menstrually unclean she deters him from coming too close in his search for the *terafim;* she actually sits upon them. The fertility-related taboo power found in every woman serves as a deception to mask her thievery.[36]

The deception is only partially uncovered. Laban reaches Jacob and family, but the gods are not recovered nor the one responsible discovered (compare the potentially tragic vow of Jacob 31:32 with that of Jepthah; this scene ends comically). The heroes, moreover, do not depart like tricksters and thieves after the encounter with Laban but are, in a sense, made respectable, institutionalized by Laban's acknowledgment, however grudging, that his flocks and daughters are now in Jacob's hands (31:43). The scene of peacemaking in 31:44–54 confirms this newly found status. In the larger tale of maturation, the trickster is becoming a different sort of hero, one more at home in the establishment. He sets out to take his place in the land of his fathers, very much like an Odysseus, but first comes a final passage, one last test of his ability to survive. Jacob sends word to Esau, divides up his camp in the hopes that some will survive a possible attack, and then sends a generous gift ahead to his brother.

Much has been written about the transformational, passage-making qualities of the wrestling scene of Genesis 32.[37] Jacob is alone, having crossed the river Jabbok (32:23–25). His literal "crossing" presages this crossing point in his life. Themes of wrestling and prevailing are contained within the folk etymology for the new name that the hero, transformed, receives from his opponent (32:29)[38] and themes of closeness to God and of survival contained within his own naming of the place where the experience takes place (32:31). These themes are central to the tale of Jacob the trickster. Jacob the trickster, evoking other cultures' Prometheus and Loki, is able momentarily to contain a power infinitely greater than he. He does not leave the confrontation unscathed, but he survives, momentarily partaking of the divine. And this Jacob, struggler, prevailer, survivor, is Israel. Tales of the trickster Jacob are, indeed, central to Israelite identity and self-image, an identity with which the prophet Hosea is none too comfortable (Hos. 12:4–6), and understandably so. Implicit in the tales of Jacob trickster, as in all trickster tales, is a lack of respect for authority. Jacob has flouted the authority of his father, his elder brother, his maternal uncle and father-in-law, and, ultimately, the authority of God. After the theophany in 28:12 ff. Jacob makes a vow to accept Yahweh as his god, with conditions. In chapter 32, Jacob wrestles with God and wrenches a blessing out of him (32:27), much as he extracted a blessing from his unwilling father (chap. 27). And yet even in the wrestling with the divine man one sees signs of a trickster in transition, for Jacob gains his blessing not through disguise, deception, or trickery but through direct confrontation and victory. In an equally direct, though conciliatory, fashion Jacob greets Esau. Instead of a trickster, Esau meets a generous reconciliator. In fact, the two men outdo one another in offers of peace and friendship. The brief scene is a necessary resolution of family rivalry, essential to complete one portion of Jacob's life. Brother rivalry is balanced by embrace; the exile's tale ends with his return.[39] The Jacob of 33:17–20, with emphases on settlement, land buying, and altar building, is reminiscent of Odysseus at the very end of Homer's tale and Gilgamesh in the "Standard Babylonian" version (Tablet XI, 303–7).[40]

The remainder of the Jacob life is found in Genesis 33–36 and in the Joseph life that follows. As it is for his father Isaac, the denouement of Jacob's life is the story of his senescence. In the life of the trickster, "institutionalization," maturity, and adulthood is followed by impotence and decline. The blind Isaac who dies at 35:29 is paralleled by the weak father of Genesis 34, unable to control his sons or to rely on their respect.

The rape of Dinah is a fine piece, evoking major sociological and anthropological issues such as exogamy and endogamy and the treatment of women and raising politicohistorical questions concerning relations with "Shechemites" and the early tribal status of Levi and Simeon. In the tale of Jacob, Genesis 34 reveals the powerlessness of Jacob. He has become the sensible reconciliator (34:30) while his children have become tricksters, convincing the Shechemites that their circumcision would be followed by peaceful treaty relations then attacking them as they recuperate from the operation.

Morphology	In Genesis 34
Uncertain status	Marginalization of Dinah as rape victim, insult to her family
Trickery/deception	Convince Shechemites to circumcise selves, promising good relations
Uncovering of deception	Attack and slaughter of Shechemites; vengeance
Status remains uncertain	They save honor but damage relations with non-Israelites of land

Genesis 34 has much to do with generations. The youths, Hamor's son and Jacob's sons, are hotheaded, active, and aggressive; the old men, Jacob and Hamor, are interested in trade, making peace, and the formation of treaties. Reuben's usurpation of Jacob's concubine Bilhah (35:22) contributes further to the image of Jacob as senescent.[41] Yet the trickster will not be the ideal of the next generation. Joseph matures into a court wise man, a quintessential member of the establishment, and though the trickster becomes a powerless old man, the wise man grows stronger and more powerful with age.

Joseph

In contrast to Jacob's quick scene of reconciliation with his rival brother, events necessary for reconciliation in the Joseph narrative begin in chapter 42, with a climax in chapter 45 and additional aspects of resolution covering a few more chapters.[42] We have discussed the delay mechanisms by which the author creates tension and drama, building to the revelation that Pharaoh's chief aide is the brother Joseph; Joseph's dream has come true, the destiny of the younger son fulfilled. The patterning of content in this important section of the Joseph narrative recalls patterns in the Jacob account and in earlier portions of the Joseph account, but with important nuances. Whereas in the Jacob account the journeys are long enough to include important theophanies and transformations and the brother reconciliation brief, in the Joseph tale all journeys, Joseph's and the brothers', are covered in one line, and the scenes with the brothers are lengthy. For the author of the Joseph account, the victory of the underdog is strung out, savored, the power of God's prediction via dreams overtly felt; Joseph remembers his dream as his brothers stand before him. In part this difference is a matter of style, as Gunkel has noted. The author of the Joseph story tends to lengthen climactic and emotional scenes. The author also artistically balances the key scene of the rivalry motif with the commencement of the resolution of rivalry.

Rivalry enacted	*Resolution enacted*
Father sends Joseph out (37:14)	Father sends brothers out (42:1–2)
Brothers see him coming (37:18)	Joseph recognizes brothers; they do not know him (42:7, 8)
Entrapment of him (37:19 ff.)	His entrapment of them via planting money (42:25)
They are temporarily in control, (so they think)	Joseph is in control

Undergirding these expressions of rivalry and beginnings of resolution is the recurring morphology: marginal status; "manipulation" (treachery/entrapment); alteration in status (with nuances).

The brothers are, of course, experiencing the same pattern of events Joseph did at their hands and at the hands of Potiphar's wife. They are manipulated and passive. Their pit/prison is to live with the horrified father who has lost another son and then again to have to choose between famine and the Egyptians. Simeon literally does become an exiled prisoner, as Joseph was:

Morphology	For Joseph
Marginal status	Though successful, he is a dead person to his family; the dream of dominance is yet unfulfilled
Entrapment/deception	Joseph's hiding his identity and planting the money in sacks
Discovery (partial)	Money found, but Joseph's identity is still hidden
Return to original status/delay	Joseph bides his time

The pattern is repeated a second time with another entrapment, the cup in Benjamin's sack, this time followed by full revelation of the truth and Joseph's complete demarginalization. He is recognized to exist and assumes rightful status over his elder brothers.

What sort of character is Joseph? Is he no better than his brothers or Potiphar's wife in assuming a comparable role in the same morphology? Or is he the wise man because his acts of entrapment accomplish their goals in the long run? Is he then a successful trickster in the end and not a wise man? There is, of course, a boundary where the two roles meet. And yet the image of Joseph as wise man remains fully intact by the end of the tale; in fact, it is strengthened. In this I disagree both with Donald Redford's suggestion that Joseph is too emotional, too angry and vengeful, to be a wise man and with Coats's description of Joseph as a despot unconcerned with his prey who contrasts with the wise counselor of chapters 39–41.[43] Redford is imagining here more the evenness of a Buddhist saint than the characteristics of one who succeeds at court.

Joseph turns aside to weep during the encounter with the brothers (42:24; 43:30; 45:2), each time growing more emotional, in accordance with the building style of the author. Joseph's emotions, however, never interfere with his weaving webs that lead to his own glorification. Moreover, Joseph's acts of entrapment are acts of just revenge, in contrast to the actions of his brothers or Potiphar's wife. Literarily, the narrative pattern, in its orderly way, must be worked out to echo and reverse the effects of the treachery committed at the beginning of the tale.[44] As we saw earlier, the narrative pattern in its typology parallels the will of God; it also underscores Joseph's role as wise man. Just revenge and self-glorification through the successful manipulation of unjust fools are all found in works such as Esther and Ahiqar, which portray the wise men at court. As Talmon and von Rad have shown, Joseph acts in accordance with courtly wisdom, knowing when to be silent (to his brothers), when to speak (41:33: he virtually recommends himself to Pharaoh), when to feign anger (42:9; 44:15), and how to please a king, being loyal to the hand that feeds him (39:9) and ever mindful of his own abilities (45:8–9) and limitations (41:16).[45] In fact, a sign of Joseph's maturation is that he now knows not to be so honest all the time. Emotion is not the mark of the fool, unless it leads to indiscretion; nor is self-confidence, unless it leads to overconfidence, hubris, and seduction by flattery. Herein lie the differences between Haman and Mordecai, Vashti and Esther, and the brothers and Potiphar's wife and Joseph.

Completing the resolution is the reunion with the father (46:29), the settling into Goshen with permission from Pharaoh (47:1–13), further tales of Joseph's success as manager to Pharaoh (47:13 ff.), the blessing of Joseph's sons (chap. 48), Jacob's final words to his sons (49:1–32),[46] and finally, at 49:33 ff., the death of Jacob and his burial, and at 50:26 the death of Joseph himself.

Joseph the wise man is never described in decline. The only hint of the senescence of the hero is when, true to the traditional literary pattern and contrary to the expectations of Joseph as father, Jacob blesses the younger son rather than the elder. This provides a faint echo of the success of the younger son.

The resolution events of the Joseph tale strongly emphasize positive attitudes to authority figures. God's authority, Pharaoh's authority, and Jacob's authority are all fully respected. Joseph obeys the old man's wishes in granting the right of primogeniture to Ephraim, the younger. He never wrestles with God in any sense. Pharaoh, like Abimelech of Genesis 20, is a benevolent figure who respects God's power. Most interesting of all, there is no negative assessment of Joseph's complete subjugation and devastation of the Egyptian people on behalf of Pharaoh during the famine.

Redford and others have suggested that Genesis 47:13 ff. reflects either an etiology for Egyptian land distribution of a certain period and/or Israelite pleasure at Egyptian suffering.[47] As in Genesis 12, the Israelite exile gains ascendancy over Egyptians. The Joseph story, however, exhibits little of the us-them quality one might expect vis-à-vis Egyptians; the monarch is not portrayed in even as negative a light as the duped lord of Genesis 12. One might interpret Genesis 47:13 ff. as reflecting a more general attitude to political authority, a positive one that contrasts with the antiestablishment nuances of trickster tales. It is acceptable for Joseph to grind Egyptians into poverty for his king's sake (contrast the prophetic tale of Naboth's vineyard, 1 Kings 21). In contrast to Genesis 12:10–20 and the Jacob-Laban tales, the Joseph tale deals not with theft of the rich man's wealth but with ingratiation, with joining and enjoying the benefits of the establishment. Again the parallel with Genesis 20 presents itself.

Conclusions from Patterning

Linking and intertwining the Jacob and Joseph tales is the overriding theme of status, the maintenance, lowering, or increasing of status, concerns at the heart of all underdog and trickster tales. The essential pattern of marginal-status/manipulation/new-status and variations upon it dominate both works, the manipulation taking the form of deception, trickery, treachery, enticement, or cleverness.

Extremely useful throughout has been attention to point of view. The story explored from one character's point of view reveals a pattern somewhat different from the story told from another's viewpoint. We have asked whose viewpoint is determinant in this or that episode, who is in control of the action, and, in this way, have learned a great deal about the odyssey and maturation of each hero. We have explored also how one work spends much time on a motif of the hero pattern and the other hardly any, and to what ends—for example, the journey and the resolution in Jacob and Joseph tales.

With the outline of the hero pattern as guide we have entered each broad motif to explore Israelite expressions of it, suggesting where each tale exhibits cross-culturally identifiable pieces of content and patterns of content and the special recurring forms of Israelite literature. The layering approach, which distinguishes between generic, specific, and typological motifs, has allowed us to explore narrative content at various levels or planes, better to examine the compositional and character interests that distinguish the authors of the Jacob and Joseph narratives. Our study strongly confirms the feasibility of a composition-critical treatment of each work and points to the varying expectations reflected in and affecting each.

The narrative patterns of both works display fine symmetry and balance. Suggestions that the Jacob tale is more episodic and choppy than the Joseph tale are challenged by this study as well as by those of Hendel, Fishbane, Fokkelman, and de Pury. Indeed, comparisons between the Joseph narrative and the Turkish tale "The Blind Patishah" remind us that even a rather typical folktale may be quite complex, having, in Propp's terms, many different moves, many different definable morphologies within the one tale. The Jacob tale, in its narrative symmetry, is no more complete without the reconciliation with

Esau than is the Joseph tale without its reconciliation. The wholeness and interlocking quality of the Jacob story is implicit in the repeated morphological pattern of the trickster that characterizes so many episodes, in the structural parallels and balance between episodes on a more typological level (see the table on p. 108), and in the overall expectations of the hero pattern. Wholeness in the Joseph story is made more explicit by overt literary foreshadowing (e.g., "but his father kept the matter in mind," 37:11) and allusion ("and Joseph remembered the dreams . . .," 42:9) often expressed by the narrator. The means of patterning in the tale of Joseph is more elaborate, even decorative, in consonance with the baroque, elaborative use of language. In the Jacob tale, the patterns themselves do the connective work, without the aid of direct narrator's signals, hints, and reminders. Each style has its own elegance and is appropriate to its hero.

Joseph, an innocent youth with mantic talents, matures into a court wise man, winning a position of power in the establishment that he maintains until his death. Jacob, an antiestablishment trickster, matures into a more institutionalized figure who declines into senescence much as did his own father. Appropriate to roles of wise man and trickster are alternative views of authority and alternative settings. The Joseph tale, set largely at court with nuances of court bureaucracy and professional dream interpretation, has a thoroughly positive portrait of authority and a cosmopolitan outlook—exogamy is fully acceptable—whereas the Jacob tale, set in the family, has a more parochial outlook—marriage among family members is much preferred. It deals with challenges to all sorts of claims to authority, especially those of the older generation. The God of the trickster is similarly challenged, himself a figure like quicksilver who appears and recedes. The God of Joseph is a steady, guiding presence throughout.

Can we draw some conclusions about the date of these works, their settings in time and place, on the basis of our study? First, one can match up the Jacob account with Genesis

12 and the Joseph tale with Genesis 20, as did Hermann Gunkel some eighty years ago. Rather than write in terms of evolution, the latter later than the former, however, one may write of popular and courtly literature that would have appealed throughout Israel's history. It is tempting to suggest that the Joseph account was composed in the heyday of one of the successful northern kings—an Omride perhaps—by an author anxious to glorify the ancestor hero of the northern tribes. The author emphasizes respect for secular authority and is at home in a baroque courtly setting. We are here imagining the roots of courtly wisdom to be deep and ancient, ultimately related to a less specialized folk wisdom manifested all over the world.

The Jacob cycle is more difficult to date. It is a founding myth of sorts, given that Jacob is "Israel," yet founding myths are retold in each generation. Jacob and Joseph tales both display strong interest in questions of status and in the cleverness or God-given wisdom that leads to high status. Thus, variations on a recurring morphology most simply described as status/manipulation/status characterize both tales. We have explored the boundary where the trickster meets the wise man and have shown how both tales contrast the wise with the foolish. As Scripture now stands, with the tale of the son interweaving and continuing the life of the father, one receives an implicit message about the successful underdog. The "new" generation is that of the wise man, for even tricksters in old age must become wise men of sorts. The wise man is a more durable hero, if a less exciting one. He is certainly the star of the piece of postexilic literature to which we now turn.

5. Esther: Folklore, Wisdom, Feminism, and Authority

It is appropriate to follow the study of the Joseph narrative with a study of Esther, for several scholars suggest that the two narratives are associated by virtue of shared literary form[1] and/or by direct interdependence through borrowing.[2] Though Rosenthal and Gan base arguments for Esther's dependence on portions of the Joseph narrative largely on linguistic similarities, Arndt Meinhold bases his case for dependence on correspondence between patterns of content.[3]

Meinhold's comparative charts reveal a variety of weaknesses. As Berg notes, Meinhold is guilty of superimposing patterns on the tales, reordering "the sequence of verses in each story to conform them to his delineation of structures."[4] It is questionable, moreover, whether in content and structural function his motifs really do correspond at the detailed level suggested by Meinhold. Genesis 40:14, 20, 23; 41:9–13, the outcome of Joseph's dream interpretation and the baker's remembering him to Pharaoh, is for Meinhold the same in its narrative role as Esther 4:1–5:8; 6:14–7:6; 8:3–6, Mordecai's mourning and communicating with Esther about Ahasuerus' decree and Esther's revelations and requests to Ahasuerus. All are listed by Meinhold as "activity of hero to ward off danger."[5] The Genesis passage has to do with Joseph's rise but is not precisely action to avoid danger. Some motifs, moreover, are described with a certain degree of detail, for example, "activity of hero to ward off danger," whereas others are quite general, "proof of constancy." Some are major items in the plot, for example, "elevation"; some mere details of denouement, "cause for success is recognized."[6] Meinhold's study is not without merit and does touch upon some key comparisons. Its weaknesses, however, point to the dangers of superimposing external patterns on literature, to the importance of exploring motifs at various degrees of specificity, and to the value of dividing a complex story such as Esther into its various episodes. Meinhold's chartings are rough-hewn and, as Berg notes, do not confirm a theory of dependency.[7] The chartings, however, begin to hint at the workings of a shared tradition of story telling. So, too, Rosenthal's examples of linguistic dependence. It is difficult to speak of formulas in our limited corpus (see the discussion in chapter 1). Nevertheless, to the folklorist, the parallel language describing the heroes' elevation at Genesis 41:42–43 and Esther 6:11 and describing the king's making a party at Genesis 40:20 and Esther 1:3; 2:18; 8:2 is suggestive of the traditional ways in which a composer describes comparable images in tales with comparable content.[8] Note that the parallel language is not precisely the same language, as one would expect with copying or borrowing, but shows flexible variation on comparable language and syntax. Such is the sign of traditional-style composition. Other examples of shared terms, phrases, or syntax point to the gray area where idiom meets formula. Thus, annoying, haranguing harassment at Genesis 39:10 and Esther 3:4—*wayhî kĕdabbĕrāh 'el yôsēp yôm yôm*, "though she spoke with Joseph day in day out"; *wayhî bĕ'āmrām 'ēlāw yôm wāyôm*, "though they spoke with him day in day out"—finds another variation in the lament at Psalm 42:11—*bĕ'āmrām 'ēlay kol hayyôm*, "in their saying to me all day long."

The language and content that Esther shares with the Joseph narrative confirms its place in the traditional-style literature of Israel. The Book of Esther also should be viewed within a wider range of traditional-style literature. In fact, of the narratives explored thus far, the Book of Esther appears the most obvious candidate for folkloristic approaches. Its characters seem to be drawn from a veritable motif index of treacherous villains, fair maidens of lowly status who become wives of kings, upright and wise heroes, stupid and ineffectual kings. Its magiclike setting is plush with the trappings of court: servants, purple furnishings, fetes, food, and magnificent clothing. Its literary patterns follow well-worn models at generic, morphological, and typological levels, patterns found in the tales of Abraham, Jacob, and Joseph and sharing much with the tales of other cultures.

Esther places in bold relief themes implicit in our studies of the wife-sister tales and the lives of Jacob and Joseph: (1) the view of authority (often unjust authority) and relations to it and related questions concerning (2) the place of women in Israelite worldview (What is women's relation to authorities, divine and human?) and (3) the attitude of Israelites to the outside, non-Israelite world.

An exploration of these sociologically and anthropologically based questions, together with a study of style and structure, lead, of course, to suggestions about authors and audiences for whom Esther is meaningful and to the continuing critique of some traditional scholarly assumptions. One is also led to interesting conclusions concerning the social ethics of Scripture vis-à-vis legitimate and illegitimate authority, conclusions holding significance for later appropriators of the biblical tradition.

Style

Esther evidences a distinctive comic-hyperbolic style beautifully appropriate to its content, tone, and themes.[9] The comic-hyperbolic style shares much with the sort of traditional-style writing found in Genesis 12 and the Jacob narrative, but also evidences some of the more expansive, ornate, or baroque touches found in Genesis 20 and the Joseph tale. In style, as in content, the Book of Esther is traditional with a twist.

One occasionally finds in Esther sentence constructions worthy of modern-day bureaucratese:

And when arrived the turn of Esther daughter of Abihayil, uncle of Mordecai who took [her] to himself as a daughter, to go to the king . . . (2:15)

Such sentences are not usual in the Book of Esther, however, which more often exhibits the brief, sometimes parallelistic, phrase-by-phrase constructions typical of the other biblical narratives we have explored.

And the king became very angry
and anger burned in him. (1:12)

See also 2:17; 2:23; 3:8; 3:15; 6:8 for other good examples. This brief phrase style encapsules a wonderful image of "fiddling while Rome burns" at 3:15:

The courtiers went in haste at the king's command
and the decree was issued in Susa, the capital.
The king and Haman settled into drinking
while the city of Susa sat dumbfounded.

This style serves to contrast the seriousness of what has happened with the portrait of apathy and petty self-absorption. The powerful parallel phrases at 4:1 in turn contrast Mordecai's response of horror, mourning, and panic with the self-satisfaction of the perpetrators of evil just seen at their drinking (4:1):

When Mordecai realized all that had been done,
he ripped his clothing
and dressed in sackcloth and ashes.
He went forth into the midst of the city
and cried out a great and bitter cry.

Traditional-style repetition is found frequently in Esther. There are ways to describe the king's accepting a suggestion by courtiers (1:21; 2:4),[10] to describe his formally allowing someone to enter his presence (4:11; 5:2; 7:4), and to indicate the sending of court decrees (3:12–13; 8:9–10). The king's recalling the assassination plot is reported in very much the same language at 6:2 as the plot was described at 2:21. The king's effusive promise to Esther that she ask and it will be granted is phrased in the same way at 5:3, 6; 7:2; 9:12. The frame of Esther's response is also found at 5:4; 5:8; 7:3; 9:13, but whereas "if it please the king" introduces an invitation to dinner in the first two instances, at 7:3 it introduces a request that her life and her people's existence be spared, and at 9:12 a request that Haman's sons be hanged. The use of the formulaic frame makes the request to be spared all the more dramatic, highlighting the climactic moment of revelation in the narrative. It makes the response to the request for vengeance the more inevitable as the tale's theme of just deserts unfolds. Similarly, language of the decree that the Jews be "destroyed, killed, and annihilated" (3:13) appears in Esther's revelation to Ahasuerus (7:4) and in the counterdecree that the Jews in turn may destroy their enemies (8:11). In a situation of reversal, this repeated language of destruction effectively creates irony, underscoring the theme of just deserts.

The dense repetition in 6:3, 6, 7, 8, 9, 10, 11 (language of dressing in royal clothing, wanting to honor, setting a person to ride on a horse) is essential to the ironic scene in which the king asks Haman's advice about the ways to honor a hero. The king, of course, is planning Mordecai's elevation in thanks for his having foiled a plot to kill the king. Haman, however, thinks the honor is to be his and makes suggestions for bestowing honor appropriately fulsome. When it turns out that the honor is to be paid to Mordecai, Haman and Mordecai essentially change places. Whereas Mordecai had been in ashes and away from court (4:1), Haman now dresses in mourning and absents himself (6:12). The prediction of Haman's wife, Zeresh, further marks this turning point in the narrative. Dense repetition enhances the irony of the situation in chapter 6, building the puffed-up Haman for his fall and involving the reader, a "fly on the wall" who is fully cognizant of Haman's self-delusion while Haman himself is ignorant. This form of repetition is strongly reminiscent of that of Genesis 39, where the seductress accuses Joseph of being the seducer. It is a baroque, hyperbolic form of repetition rather than evidence of economical style.

Economical style is not always the norm in Esther. For example, in two places where one would expect traditional-style repetition, one finds instead abbreviated allusion. The maidens tell Esther about Mordecai's condition briefly (4:4), not employing the description of 4:1. Similarly, 4:7, 8 is a much briefer version of 3.9 ff. Mordecai reports to Esther "all that happened," not what happened in traditional style, that is, fully. Compare Rebecca's reports to Jacob about the words of Isaac and the plans of Esau. Thus, though Esther evidences fine traditional style, it evidences also the sort of elaborative touches characteristic of the Joseph narrative and the tendencies to summarize typical of nontraditional-style literature.

The most distinctive feature of style in Esther is the extensive use of elaborative chains of synonyms, the tendency to say precisely the same thing two, three, or four times. This is the parallel style of Hebrew narration pushed to the hyperbolic, a style entirely appropriate to the exaggerated extremes of good and evil, wise and foolish, imminent destruction turned to instant salvation found in Esther.

Thus we have the full lists of seven eunuchs and seven princes in 1:10 and 1:14. The king plans not merely to kill the Jews but *lĕhašmîd lahărōg ûlĕʾabbēd*, "to destroy, to kill, and to cause to perish" (so 7:4 and 8:11). The people's mourning is described, *wĕṣôm ûbĕkî ûmispēd śaq wāʾēper*, "and fasting, and weeping, and wailing, sackcloth and ashes . . ." (4:3), and the kitchen sink for good measure. Esther asks that the people fast over her and not eat and not drink (4:16). The rejoicing at 8:16 is described, "for the Jews there was light and rejoicing, joy and honor." They are to celebrate *bĕkol dôr wādôr mišpāḥāh ûmišpāḥāh mĕdînāh ûmĕdînāh wĕʿîr wāʿîr*, "in every generation, every family, every province, and every city" (9:28; cf. 8:17).

Esther's style, frequently economical in repetition, thus also waxes more ornate and more hyperbolic. An examination of narrative structures leads back to the underdog and the trickster, to familiar morphologies and especially to traditional-style typologies.

Status and Wisdom in Four Parts

Esther contains four major plot moves: (1) the story of Vashti's banishment, (2) the story of Esther's becoming queen, (3) the brief story of Mordecai's saving the king, (4) the most important story of Esther's saving Mordecai and her people.

Scholars have suggested that some of these "moves" are based on individual stories, perhaps specific Persian tales, borrowed and reformulated by the author of Esther.[11] Bardtke goes so far as to posit a source book of Persian tales from which the author made selections.[12] Again we encounter the image of the scholar at work in the scriptorium rather than the composer creating in a story-telling tradition. It is certainly true that any of the four plot lines could and do make for a good traditional tale, but it is equally true that folktales—even orally composed tales—are often made of combinations of such plots, as is Esther. Recall our comments on the Turkish "Blind Patishah" earlier. As Bickerman and Berg note, the Book of Esther, the whole, is beautifully balanced and unified as it now stands.[13] Others have looked for evidence of different sources in the seeming "doublets" of content, the two lists of court officials, the two banquets, and so on.[14] Such repetitions, however, are part of the traditional-style woof and warp of the tale, as are instances of repetitive, economical language. The Book of Esther divides into sources only by the most wooden exegesis. The folklorist and the composition-critic again find allies in each other.

The Fall of Vashti

The Book of Esther is about the status quo, maintenance of it, and finding a proper place within it. Vashti's actions mark her as a threat to the status quo, and she is eliminated. The "banished queen" (S416) and "banished wife" (S411) are common folk motifs appearing in various traditional typologies.

Such banishments are often of innocent women, falsely accused and later rehabilitated by their husbands. The dismissal of "arrogant" wives assumed guilty by the tradition is no less common in folklore: one thinks of the misogynistic Norwegian tale of the husband who kills his shrew wife and throws her in the river, where her body floats upstream.[15] The presence in folklore of the "uppity" wife is in itself interesting and exposes a male-chauvinist tendency shared by the author of Esther and the larger folk tradition. Gender-related issues emerge strongly in the Book of Esther. Its heroine is a woman who offers a particular model for success, one with which oppressors would be especially comfortable. Opposition is to be subtle, behind the scenes, and ultimately strengthening for the power structure. A number of modern feminist writers have, in fact, found their heroine in Vashti, their empathy with her, while regarding Esther as a weak collaborator with tyranny, an antifeminist[16]— a subject to which we will return. For the writer of Esther, however, Vashti's foolishness is the foil for Esther's wisdom, her dismissal justified and, indeed, from a narrative point of view, the spark that commences the story.

On the other hand, the man, the king who banishes Vashti, receives no sympathy from the writer. He eats, and drinks, and follows willy-nilly the advice of others. His courtiers fear that Vashti will become a model of resistance for all wives. Others have pointed justifiably to the humorous tone here; it is the humor of those in control. It is easy to laugh at a potential loss of power when there is no real threat. Vashti must be put away.

Generic	Morphological	Typological
Problem	Threat to status quo	Queen refuses to appear before king
A plan	Exercise of wisdom	Courtiers advise banishment
Resolution	Threat eliminated	Queen banished (new problem)

The king's decision to find a replacement for Vashti may be introduced here by an erotic suggestion, "the king remembered what Vashti used to do" (2:1), presumably "for him." He does not miss a person or a personality but a function. This under-lines his shallowness, of course, but the portrait of the king is fully in tune with another traditional motif, that of the stupid, impotent king. Such kings, who have something in common with the patriarchs as senexes portrayed in Genesis,[17] have no control of the situation around them. As fathers to princesses desired by dragons, they have no idea how to resist. (For other examples, see Thompson Motif J1705.4.) Thus Ahasuerus, the surface mover of the story, is a manipulated, passive tool as much as Esther is, and he remains so throughout the narrative. Again the folk character has his equivalent in what Old Tes-tament scholars generally assign to Near Eastern wisdom tra-dition. As Talmon has shown, Ahasuerus exemplifies how not to be a good ruler and wise.[18] Though the Ahasuerus of Esther is somewhat akin to the buffoon Pharaoh of Genesis 12, the portrait is much fuller here and the implicit attitude to authority more complicated. He is less respected than Joseph's Pharaoh, who at least knows enough to have good men around him, and certainly less respected than the rulers of Genesis 20 and 26, who are so ethically scrupulous. Ahasuerus may be molded; he can be made good or evil. A wise person never trusts such a leader, nor does he or she openly oppose or trick him. He is a given, and his power is a given; one must learn to make the most of the fool. Haman, Mordecai, and Esther all try their hand at controlling the king for their own advantage. In this first move the king's advisers direct him to find a new queen, and, of course, he follows their advice. The banishment of Vashti thus leads to a new problem and the story of Esther's rise.

The Rise of Esther

If one tells the story from Ahasuerus' point of view, the plot deals with the lack of a family member and the need to make the family whole, as do the birth episodes in the narratives of Jacob and Joseph; yet as the morphological outline indicates, the Book of Esther presents not merely a matter of marginal or incomplete status but of status quo interrupted:

Generic	Morphological	Typological
Problem	Status quo upset	First wife banished
Plan	Search	Beauty contest to find a new one
Resolution	Restoration of status quo	An underdog selected to become new wife

As in Genesis 20, concern with the status quo is extremely important in the Book of Esther. The work is largely about the status quo and how to become and stay a part of it. From Esther's point of view, the tale traces a familiar morphological pattern: underdog status, for Esther is an adopted orphan, a member of an exiled people instructed by her cousin not to reveal her identity as a Jew; intervention by helpers, that is, Mordecai's wise advice to keep silent (2:10) and Hegai's advice not to ask for too much (2:15); rise in status, as Esther becomes queen.

Very much like Joseph, Esther is a passive character at the beginning of her story who will become an active character later. Helpers, Mordecai and Hegai, guide her career as God guided that of Joseph. Like Joseph, she finds favor with her overlords (2:9). Her major asset is her beauty, a gift of nature. It might be suggested that as a woman, Esther does display already hints of an author's notion of the exercise of wisdom by a wise woman. She knows enough to take good advice and to be self-effacing, humble, and even-tempered. In Scripture it is noticeable that Esther's helpers are human beings and not God, but it is perfectly usual in folk narration. The morphology, as Dundes would remind us, works well no matter how the general motifs are specified.[19] A difference in the sort of helpers, however, is an important indicator of the interests of author and audience.

Most noticeable about this move in the Book of Esther,

whether explored from the point of view of the controller of the action, Ahasuerus (as much as he controls anything), or that of the one controlled, is how typical of folklore the typological motifs are at a quite specific level. Thus, the "beauty contest" by which the heroine of low status becomes royalty finds many folk parallels in Cinderella tales and their ilk (see Thompson motifs T91.6.2; T121.8). As we have shown, the details of the first two moves, characterizations, actions, and settings are quite compatible with folk literature.

Does any detail make Esther distinctive? The one thread that is distinctively Israelite is the most obvious: Esther's lowly status is largely defined by her being Jewish. Her fear to reveal her identity is most significant and points to a strong us-them quality in the work. The underdog tales explored in chapters 2–4 distinguish between haves and have-nots—those with status and wealth versus those without, those with the rights of primogeniture versus those without such rights, those with parents' love versus those without—all status issues, to be sure. In Esther, however, the clearest marker of us versus them is whether one is a Jew or not. To be Jew is to have marginal status.

Lee Humphreys, Arndt Meinhold, Shemaryahu Talmon, and others have pointed to the exilic mentality in Esther, drawing parallels between worldview in this work and in the tale of Joseph.[20] It is certainly true that Potiphar's wife describes Joseph as the Hebrew slave (Gen. 39:14, 17) and that Joseph is introduced to Pharaoh as a Hebrew (Gen. 41:12),[21] but his ethnic otherness it not strongly emphasized in the work, whereas it is central in Esther. "Hebrew" may in fact mean 'apiru, that is, "stateless person," in the Joseph story and emphasize his marginality rather than his ethnicity.[22]

The Book of Esther is indeed an early example of Jewish folk literature with important implications for the developing tradition. This emerges in "Esther's rise" and especially in the "saving of Mordecai." The most significant and final move of

Esther is preceded by another that serves as an important transition in the tale.

How Mordecai Saves the King

This typological pattern is found not only in countless traditional tales but also in popular film and television:

Generic	Morphological	Typological
Problem	Threat (to status quo)	Plot to kill king
Intervention	Exercise of wisdom	Wise man spies on perpetrators and reports them
Resolution	Threat eliminated	Perpetrators hanged

The "espionage" story is, perhaps, the modern equivalent of the court conflict/intrigue tale. As in the banishment of Vashti, the direct affront to authority leads to downfall. Mordecai's wisdom emerges not only in his loyalty but also in letting no information escape his attention, a wise activity for the courtier, as Talmon has emphasized, but also for the folk hero who succeeds by using his head. (See motif K1956.7: sham wise man utilizes overheard conversation, a trickster tale.) Again, except for the fact that Mordecai is a Jew, this tale has a stock quality. It is a necessary episode in the larger narrative; the king's recollection of Mordecai's help will commence the evil Haman's downfall.

The Saving of Mordecai and the Jews

The morphological pattern is the same as that of Mordecai's saving Ahasuerus and the fall of Vashti, but now the threat is directed against Mordecai and his people. Each of these typological elements finds parallels in Thompson's Motif Index. The Motif Index is rich in treacherous counselors (K2290), servants (K2250.1), slaves (K2251), and rivals (K2220). Haman finds a place among this traditional stock, as does his end: to be "condemned to the punishment he has suggested for others" (Q581). Themes of wisdom and lack of wisdom again intertwine with folkloristic characterizations, for tales about wise and foolish are narrative manifestations of folk wisdom. In this case, wisdom is offered for dealing with persons of higher status.

Generic	Morphological	Typological
Problem	Threat	Evil courtier seeks to eliminate rival and rival's nation and convinces the king to assist him
Intervention	Exercise of wisdom	Queen cleverly reveals matters to king and changes his mind
Resolution	Elimination of threat	King's orders altered, perpetrator hanged, and enemies defeated in reversal of evil courtier's plans

Haman's obsequiousness to the queen, his advice giving, are attempts to appear the good and wise counselor, but his self-absorption, his overwhelming self-love grounded in insecurity, mark him as the fool and as evil, which, as the Rabbis note, is often the same thing. The combination of a foolish king and a villainous adviser makes for special mischief. Ahasuerus is oblivious to the rivalries around him and presumably unconcerned that the Mordecai who saved him is a Jew threatened by Haman's proposed edict of annihilation.

Esther, though initially guided and motivated by her cousin (4:8, 13–14), finally becomes an independent wisdom heroine. She invites the king and Haman to two dinner parties, revealing her own identity and exposing the villain at the second of these. The queen "intervening for a condemned courtier" is found in Thompson's Motif Index (P21), as is the daughter who intercedes with the king to save her father.[23] Esther's cleverness emerges in the way she employs womanly wiles to seduce Haman and Ahasuerus to wisdom. Like a Judith or an Abigail, Esther dresses for success; she speaks in sweet words of flattery and is self-effacing in demeanor ("if it please the king . . ."). Like these women, she employs wine and good food to set up her situation, reaching a man through his stomach. In short, she is an altogether appealing portrait of women's wisdom for the men of a ruling patriarchate, but hardly an image meaningful or consoling to modern women. She is, as such, not peculiar to Israelite imagery, nor to Near Eastern or biblical "wisdom" traditions, but fully typological, reminding us nevertheless of the ways in which traditional literature reflects and affects a prevailing culture. This sort of tale is about maintenance of status quo, about working from within the system, and serves to reinforce such values. Esther contrasts with the rash Vashti, who would insolently and overtly dare to challenge a king in direct contradiction to the advice of folk wisdom.

The narrative goes to great lengths, in fact, to show that it is not only Esther who is "wise" in this self-effacing sense but all the Jews. To be wise is to be a good citizen. Haman's charges of Jewish rebelliousness and tricksterism are refuted, for Mordecai saved his king; Esther wins the king over not by confrontation but by begging for her life.[24] The Jews defend themselves only because they have the king's permission to fight! (Esther 8:11–12). They fight a just war, killing only in proportion to that plotted against them, taking no booty. Not taking booty not only evokes holy war theology but also underscores the non-self-aggrandizing and defensive nature of the war. In Robert Gordis's translation of 8:11, the Jews are not about to slaughter their enemies' children, wives, and so on but to defend themselves against those who are about to slaughter the Jews' children.[25] His suggestion could be correct, but even if the more usual translations of 8:11 are correct, Jewish vengeance in Esther does not reflect a debased spirit peculiar to "postprophetic Israel," that is, to Judaism, or evidence Jewish "ethnocentricism," as some would suggest.[26] Drawing parallels with events in 1916 Russia, Gunkel considers the Book of Esther to be about the first pogrom against the Jews.[27] It is ironic that such a work has been the target of misunderstandings. These insensitive descriptions of Esther fail, at any rate, to appreciate its folk-literary qualities. Folktales of Esther's type go this way; violence rounds out a theme of just deserts. (See motif Q581:*lex talionis*.) What is remarkable about the Jacob and Joseph narratives is that a violent conclusion to a pattern of rivalry between brothers is avoided; these underdog tales are family narratives with messages of wholeness and healing. Esther deals with a stronger theme about us and them, insiders and outsiders, and the traditional pattern goes as one would expect. It is no coincidence that all the wise and good characters in Esther are Jews, the foolish, rash, and evil ones non-Jews. Esther is a strongly ethnic tale. Even so, the message of this victory of "us" over "them" is a careful, cautious one that does not advocate direct and open rebellion against injustice—quite the contrary. One begins to see that Esther is not only about wise and foolish, good and evil but also about attitudes to authority and methods of dealing with unjust authority,[28] central questions in Jewish ethics as old as the founding myth tradition of the Exodus.

Underdog Tales and Social Ethics

The response of the Book of Esther to injustice has implications not only for Jews' relations with an often hostile world but also for women's relationship to Judaism. The Book of Esther encourages attempts to work from within the system, to become an indispensable part of it. This model personified by Esther is strongly contrasted with that of Vashti. Direct resistance fails.

The trickster and the wisdom hero/heroine have much in common: the stealthy, home-based power of the women; the emphasis on clever, behind-the-scenes manipulation of those of higher status to secure for oneself benefits. And yet the trickster tales have a clear antiestablishment bent. Tricksters toy with the establishment and when uncovered escape, elude authority, and trick again. They embody chaos, marginality, and indefinability. The wisdom heroes and heroines seek to become a part of the system that threatens them and, like Esther and Joseph, enjoy being a part of the establishment, deriving much benefit from it. They personify order, neatness, a world in which everything fits.[29]

How does one evaluate this model for and of dealing with unjust authority? Some in later Jewish tradition are rather uncomfortable with Esther. Whereas Judith can brag (over and over) that the heathen Holophernes never laid a hand on her, Esther cannot be so proud about her accomplishments. Hence the Zohar's suggestion that Esther never lay with Ahasuerus, for God would send a female spirit to the king in her place (Zohar III, 275b–276b). Clearly, the folktale writer has no qualms about women's using sexuality to obtain benefits for themselves or others. The later exegetical tradition shows some ambivalence. Some of the Rabbis praise Vashti for her resistance, suggesting that the hedonistic Ahasuerus had wanted Vashti to dance naked before his friends (Esther Rabbah 3:13–14). The Rabbis, of course, are not proponents of women's liberation. Much as the Moral Majority and the National Organization for Women might agree on issues of pornography, so the Rabbis appear to take a feminist position. Nevertheless, the issue of unjust authority is raised. Fine studies such as David Daube's *Collaboration with Tyranny* explore this issue in rabbinic political ethics.[30] Relations to unjust authority remain hotly debated issues in post-Holocaust Judaism. Interesting for our purposes is that the underdog tales provide various models for dealing with authority: tricksterism, self-inclusion in the power-structure, and/or collaboration. Were tales of Samson and

David included in our study we could add another: direct confrontation.

Author and Audience

Where does our study of Esther—its style, structures, and themes—lead in dealing with questions of author and audience? Do the concerns of the folklorist lead us away from answers of traditional biblical scholarship concerning the date and provenance of Esther?

Style in Esther does not provide as clear a guide as it does in Genesis 12 and 20 or the Jacob narrative and Joseph narrative. A style that is quite traditional combines with baroque nuances to produce a style all its own, characterized in particular by hyperbolic chains of synonyms. It may well be that in Esther, distinctions of "courtly" versus "popular" style relevant for a preexilic or early postexilic Palestinian setting have no meaning. We are clearly dealing with postmonarchic literature and probably with non-Palestinian Jewish literature.[31]

It is not surprising that scholars who have been most sensitive to the folk quality of Esther's content and structure—for example, Gaster and Bickerman—have been least willing to find in Esther hints of specific Persian period history.[32] Other scholars have employed archaeological information from the excavations at Susa to suggest that details in the work are historical;[33] Ungnad published a cuneiform text mentioning Marduka, a high official of the Susa court during the reign of Xerxes I.[34] Claus Schedl attempts further to argue away problems in Esther such as the age of Mordecai, who would have been about 150 years old in the time of Ahasuerus-Xerxes—if deported in the time of Nebuchadnezzar.

Talmon describes the consensus of scholarly opinion thus:

The author of the Esther-story generally shows an intimate knowledge of Persian court-etiquette and public administration. He must have had some personal experience of these matters or else was an extremely well-informed and gifted writer.[35]

The author of the Book of Esther does employ Persian local color, Persian names and words, a setting in Susa, and mention of court personnel and is aware of the setup of the Persian kingdom in provinces and so on, but I question whether this sort of knowledge is intimate or based on personal experience at court. A Persian period date seems logical; it is from this setting that the author draws local color, but it would not have been necessary to be of the court to do so.

Talmon reads into the text one example of Esther's realistic portrayal of the counselors attached to Near Eastern courts when he suggests that Mordecai and Haman are portrayed as multilingual and thus modeled after real court officials.[36] The language these men speak may be as irrelevant to the audience of the Esther tale as the fact that Frenchmen in 1948 war films always speak to one another in English with Austrian accents.[37] We suspend disbelief about these matters when participating in narrative experiences.

Zeroing in on the date of court wisdom portrayals in Esther, Talmon suggests further that the wisdom heroine is a uniquely biblical phenomenon in the ancient Near East until possibly the Persian period.[38] The commonness of wise women in plots such as those of Esther in world folklore casts suspicion both upon the uniqueness of Esther in the Near East and upon her relation to Persian motifs of a particular period. The same must be said of the suggestion that the Book of Esther reveals "the courtier-counselor's psychology."[39] It is a wisdom tale in which underdogs succeed via proverbial wisdom exercised at court, but are comparable wisdom tales filled with powerful dupes, wise women, and themes of just deserts always from a courtier-class author?[40]

Finally, folklore, the literature and the field, cautions us to be careful in our descriptions of wisdom literature as a genre. Many of the traits Talmon finds in wisdom works—for example, the ad-hoc mentality and lack of historical depth, the undeveloped characterizations[41]—scholars such as Olrik and Lüthi claim to find in a whole range of folklore.[42] Does Talmon observe the wisdom quality of the Book of Esther or its folk-loristic quality?

Thus although Esther certainly is about the wise and the fool-ish, about wisdom as the means to succeed and become a member of the "ruling class," and though it does have a court set-ting and strongly Persian local color, it need not have been composed by a member of a courtly elite, as Meinhold sug-gests;[43] nor is it easily assignable to one period in Persian his-tory, as others suggest.[44]

An important indicator of Esther's author and audience is its attitude to authority as part of a larger worldview. In this con-text one might also explore suggestions that a historical kernel is to be found in the escape of the Jewish community from a threat to its very existence.[45]

It is as impossible to ascertain whether or not this escape has a historical kernel as it is to answer the same question about the exodus. We can say for Esther, as Gerleman has noticed, that the people's narrow escape from oppressors in exile is a favorite, indeed central, Israelite literary *typos*.[46] It is through this specification of cross-culturally found narrative patterns, the threat morphology and the evil courtier typology, that the Jewish author makes this work meaningful to an audience, giv-ing it special power of identification for the reality of a people caught in a particular historical and sociological setting.

I am inclined to believe that the work was written in dias-pora, for a cultural group surrounded by overlords in an alien setting, for a minority rather than for a conquered and cultur-ally threatened majority in Palestine. In this I agree with Hum-phreys, Meinhold, and others.[47] What mode of relating to au-thority is offered? It is the way of Jeremiah, as Humphreys notes (Jer. 29:4–7), to build homes, raise families, be good cit-izens, but more. It suggests becoming a full part of the system, all the while acknowledging the stupidity of those who run the system. We must not forget, moreover, that the Book of Esther is comedy, as Samuel Sandmel saw so well.[48] It is meant to be amusing as well as uplifting and is ultimately optimistic, if sobering. The author of Esther is more audacious and insulting to authority than the respectful author of the Joseph story, who is more likely to have written in the context of Israelite royalty than foreign lordship. The author of Esther is at the same time more accepting of authority than the authors of the trickster tales. One deals with life in exile as members of an insecure, sometimes persecuted minority by steering a course of survival somewhere between co-option and self-respect and by holding to the conviction that to be wise and to be worthy are the same. Critical also are the psychological release of humor and the enactment of ultimate vindication in lively literary and cultic traditions. The plot of the folktale, in which one knows all will turn out well for the heroes whether via their wisdom or "some other source," thus makes real suffering bearable and helps to bridge the gap between the way things are and they way they should be.

Conclusions

Underdogs and Tricksters is a study in paradigms, a search for the recurring patterns underlying stories about unlikely heroes, a case study in the application of folklore methodology to the traditional literature of the Bible, a reflection on the Israelite worldviews implicit in a set of tales about heroes and heroines providing various models for dealing with authority.

Folklore reinforces some of our best instincts as Bible scholars, the concern with "texture," the way language is used, being one critical aspect of this interdisciplinary study important both to folklorists and Scripture scholars. We have uncovered a range of styles: a popular-economical style in Genesis 12 and the Jacob narrative, a baroque-rhetorical style in Genesis 20 and the Joseph narrative, an anthological style in Genesis 26, and a comic-hyperbolic style in Esther. Other interests of folklorists have led to areas of exploration not frequented by the majority of Scripture scholars, though the work of Irvin, Culley, Long, Coote, Oden, Gunn, Polzin, Hendel, and others moves with us in one or several of these newer directions.

With its emphasis on performance, folklore leads away from notions of rote borrowing, wooden adaptation, and scholastic redaction to explain the existence of three biblical tales about the patriarch who says his wife is his sister or the similarities between tales of Joseph and Mordecai/Esther. Instead we look to composers at home in a tradition, weaving tales out of familiar narrative threads for audiences who identify with the same set of cultural assumptions. The interest in composers leads away from the search for composite sources and to the treatment of narrative wholes as they now stand. Folklore, biblical form-criticism, and composition-criticism thus meet on a boundary marked by the signpost of literary creativity circum-scribed by cultural expectation.

Folklorists' emphasis on literature-in-process and multiform-ity leads away from the search for Ur-forms in comparing the wife-sister tales or in seeking to understand why the tale about Joseph looks like the tale about Jacob. In eschewing the search for Ur-forms, in fact, we also eschew the attempt to prove that the narratives we study had an original oral form. What we can say is that the tales we have explored, their pieces of con-tent and the combinations of these pieces, exemplify a process of traditional-style composition grounded in variation on re-curring multiforms. Hence our interest in the recurring patterns of content in tales of underdogs and tricksters. In exploring "patterns" and not "genres" we avoid squeezing Old Testament tales into models provided by Icelandic sagas or European *Märchen*, allowing each tale's own motifs, patterns, and mes-sages to emerge. Our treatment of the content of the tales and their structures of content is a complex one.

Influenced by folklorists' interests in the "generic" and the "nominal," the universal and the culture-bound, the culture-bound and the composer-bound, the general and specific as-pects of so many features of narration, we have sought means of describing tales, their content and structure, at various syn-chronic levels. The "overlay map" technique employed closely in chapter 2 and more broadly in chapters 3 and 4 suggests that a narrative may be defined in lowest-common-denominator terms—for example, problem/plan/resolution, a pattern shared by an infinite array of narratives. We call this level "the ge-neric." This base level of content is specified at deeper, more detailed levels: at the specific or morphological level (the prob-lem may be the hero's marginal status), at the typological level (the hero's marginality may be expressed by his or her "lack of children"), and at the individual level (e.g., Rebecca's bar-renness).

The overlay map technique brings to the fore various struc-turalist and comparativist techniques and seeks not merely to compare stories of similar content and/or structure but to compare their content and structure at parallel planes. At the morphological level and the typological level we find congruence between the content and patterns in Israelite tales and those of distant cultures. What does recognition of that which is cross-culturally shared tell us about Israelite tradition? In what ways does an Israelite author diverge significantly from more usual forms of the story? At the individual level, what are Israelite authors' favorite expressions of common motifs cross-culturally shared at broader levels?

In contrast to many comparable tales of other cultures, the tales of Jacob and Joseph conclude brother rivalry not with violent elimination of one rival but with reconciliation. These patriarchal tales thus differ from the typologically more usual Cain and Abel story. The authors of the Jacob and Joseph tales evidence concern for the theme of wholeness and unity among members of the same clan, reflecting and buttressing a critical feature of Israelite worldview and self-image in the way they tell their stories. Also at the typological level, God's steady presence as a helper motif in Genesis 20, Genesis 26, and various episodes of the Joseph narrative contrasts with more quixotic divine appearances in Genesis 12 and the patterns of the Jacob narrative and with a virtual absence of God in Esther. A study in typology thus becomes a study in contrasting theology. At the individual Israelite and tale-specific level, we gain information about a view of women. Childlessness is not the problem of both parents, as in a Turkish tale of the same typological pattern, but always the problem of the woman. She is the conduit of fertility, lack of fertility her curse, as most graphically portrayed by the dilemma of Rachel. At the individual level, we have treated favorite Israelite literary forms as the stuff of narrative composition and placed these forms in context. The annunciation, for example, is understood as a culture-specific expression of a cross-culturally found typological motif concerning the birth of the hero.

Most important and far-reaching have been our findings at

the morphological level. Recurring over and over within individual tales and between tales is the pattern, marginal-status/exercise-of-wit/demarginalization. This pattern, the mark of many underdog tales, is not found in Genesis 20 or in Genesis 26. Though Genesis 20 shares several important motifs with Genesis 12 at the typological level, the shared motifs work out quite different morphologies. The wife-as-sister deception of Genesis 12 is instead a declaration of truth with a twist in Genesis 20, for in chapter 20 Sarah is both wife and sister to Abraham. Genesis 20 is concerned not as much with raises in status as with maintenance of the status quo, here defined as proper familial relationships. Concern with status quo of another sort applies also to the most important narrative thread of the Esther tale, the saving of the Jews.

Though Genesis 26 shares the morphological elements of marginal status and demarginalization, the markings of the underdog pattern, the link between statuses is not a human being's own efforts or individual effort aided by a helper, but direct divine intervention. The same morphological pattern is found in the tale of Jacob and Esau's birth.

All of our tales deal with status in some form, raises in low status or threats to the status quo. We might add to the variations exemplified by Genesis 20 and 26 the unsuccessful attempts by antagonists to maintain or alter their current status at the expense of our heroes via entrapment, itself a form of "wit." When narrative patterns are traced from the point of view of Joseph's brothers, Potiphar's wife, and Haman, we find an interesting counterpoint to the dominant morphology of our tales.

The center point in this dominant morphology, "wit," takes two basic forms, creating a dichotomy between wisdom and tricksterism. The wisdom hero alters status via the careful, judicious exercise of God-given gifts. Joseph is a skilled interpreter of dreams, humbly admitting that his power comes from God, serving first his father, then Potiphar, and finally Pharaoh with consummate loyalty. He is a pillar of the establishment, his success extremely durable. Like Joseph, Mordecai and Esther are cautious, good listeners knowing how to please those with authority over them. They improve their situation through wisdom.

In contrast, the Abram of Genesis 12 and the youthful Jacob are tricksters, deceiving a ruler in Abram's case, tricking a patriarch, an elder brother, and a father-in-law, wrestling and bargaining even with God in the case of Jacob. Though the exercise of their wit is not evil, neither is it wisdom. It is con-artistry and antiestablishment behavior at its best. The success of the tricksters is less stable than that of the wisdom heroes; they are often in flight—in Jacob's case, even the object of others' trickery.

The discovery of the dichotomy between tricksters and wise men may allow us to draw some conclusions about the authors and audiences within Israelite tradition, though we, like the wisdom heroes, must proceed cautiously and appreciate complexities.

Recalling that the Jacob narrative and Genesis 12 share a popular style and that the Joseph tale exhibits a baroque style, one is tempted to chart trajectories: baroque style—wisdom heroes—proestablishment attitudes—court literature; popular style—tricksters—antiestablishment attitudes—non-court literature. Portrayals of God in the contrasting works contribute further to our trajectories, for the trickster's theophanic, quixotic God contrasts with the ever-present, rather more predictable deity of the wise man. Contrasting threads in Israelite worldview and self-image offer alternative models for dealing with authority. These threads may be coterminous and ongoing, though it is interesting that the author responsible for the current form of Genesis has the wise man Joseph replace the trickster Jacob, whereas the trickster Jacob himself is portrayed as growing into a more establishmentarian elder. So do we all.

The Joseph tale is probably from a northern court setting. Dating and placement for the other material from Genesis is difficult. Where in all this does Esther fit? The next logical step may appear to be to match Esther and the Joseph tale. Certainly Esther and Mordecai succeed via wisdom; certainly they benefit from the establishment and seek to remain welcome within it. They are no tricksters. Yet the style of Esther is something between baroque and popular, its divine helper negligible, and, most important of all, its attitude to authority other than the one we have seen among tricksters or wise men—again, perhaps, somewhere in between.

In the Joseph narrative, as in Genesis 20, which in style and bent shares much with Genesis 37–50, as Gunkel once noted, monarchs are presented as benevolent, ethically upright, reasonably intelligent—worthy, in short, of their power. Pharaoh appreciates Joseph's talents, is eminently hospitable to his family and capable of following solid advice. A pious Abimelech accepts and respects God's advice and makes full restitution to Abraham on Sarah's behalf. As king's lieutenant, moreover, Joseph is portrayed as fully within his rights and the rights of the monarchy in acquiring land for the king at the expense of the people. This is the most extreme example of the message that kingship is an appropriate and proper mode of social structure. Seeming injustice is clothed in respectability. These tales reflect a mode of social structure and, indeed, validate it. I am comfortable, therefore, with suggestions for courtly or aristocratic origins for these works.

The monarch in the Book of Esther, however, is a buffoon, the typological motif of the stupid king, a dangerous, hedonistic fool, capable of being led astray by evil men and not reliably able to choose between good and bad advice. Monarchy is a reality that wise men may be able to manipulate for their own benefit, but they must remain ever suspicious. The Book of Esther evidences no respect for political authority. It is about coping with unjust authority, and its offered solution is suspicious and savvy collaboration. The morphological pattern marginal-status/wit/raised-status is operative in Esther. It describes, from Esther's point of view, her rise to become queen and Mordecai's elevation after saving the king. Equally operative, however, is the pattern threat-to-status/exercise-of-wit/status-maintained, ever threatening to reverse previous gains, to reduce the status of the Jews and to destroy them. Like tricksters, the wise men in Esther are survivors, and their success, though not grounded in con-artistry, is as unstable as that of tricksters. Their marginality is defined by their Jewishness, a condition that will not change, and their security based on the favor of a fool.

Who might have composed such a work? If Esther is a court narrative, as Talmon and others suggest, we see here the difference between the author of the Joseph narrative, an Israelite possibly writing at his own king's court, and the author of Esther, a Jew writing as an exile. Esther does exemplify a variety of wisdom lore supportive of the power structure, for it recommends working within the system even if it is unjust; such a worldview need not, however, originate at court. Esther provides one viable human response to injustice, suffering, or anomie, a means of coping with oppression. It does seem likely to have been meaningful to people who had something to gain as well as much to lose from the system. This could apply to members of any prospering Jewish community under foreign domination. Esther, in fact, is a remarkably modern piece of Jewish literature, providing a relevant model for dealing with unjust authority in the centuries subsequent to its composition. The other tales with which we have dealt provide alternative models ranging from challenge to the status quo to full collaboration.

Tales of underdogs and tricksters ultimately deal with fundamental aspects of individual and group identity, such as authority and empowerment, stasis and change. The study of traditional narrative patterns points to interconnections between the layered material of story and the patinas of human behavior. Israelite tales of unlikely heroes reflect the worldviews of a variety of authors and audiences but also provide options for modern readers and appropriators. Folklore, the field of study and the material studied, sensitizes us to the complex webs of content and meaning linking our stories and ourselves.

List of Abbreviations

AB	Anchor Bible. Garden City, N.J.: Doubleday.
AFS	American Folklore Society
ANET	*Ancient Near Eastern Texts* ed. James B. Pritchard. Princeton: Princeton University Press, 1969.
BKAT	*Biblischer Kommentar: Altes Testament.* Neukirchen-Vluyn: Neukirchener Verlag.
BR	*Biblical Research*
B st	*Biblische Studien.* Neukirchen-Vluyn: Neukirchener Verlag.
CBQ	*Catholic Biblical Quarterly*
CBQMS	Catholic Biblical Quarterly Monograph Series. Washington, D.C.: Catholic Biblical Association of America
FFC	Folklore Fellows Communications. Helsinki: Suomalainen tiedeakatemia.
HR	*History of Religions*
HTR	*Harvard Theological Review*
HUCA	*Hebrew Union College Annual*
IB	Interpreter's Bible. Nashville and New York: Abingdon Press.
IDB	*Interpreter's Dictionary of the Bible.* Nashville and N.Y.: Abingdon Press, 1962.
JAF	*Journal of American Folklore*
JBL	*Journal of Biblical Literature*
JSOT	*Journal for the Study of the Old Testament*

KAT	Kommentar zum Alten Testament. Gütersloh: Gerd Mohn.
PMLA	*Proceedings of the Modern Languages Association*
SBL	Society of Biblical Literature
TAPA	*Transactions of the American Philosophical Association.*
VT	*Vetus Testamentum*
ZAW	*Zeitschrift für die alttestamentliche Wissenschaft*
ZDMG	*Zeitschrift der deutschen morgenlandischen Gesellschaft*

Notes

Introduction

1. On oral composition, see A. B. Lord, *The Singer of Tales.*
2. See the definition of folklore by Barre Toelken, *The Dynamics of Folklore,* 32.
3. William R. Bascom, "Verbal Art"; Elli-Kaija Köngäs-Maranda, "The Concept of Folklore," 85; Frances Lee Utley, "Folk Literature: An Operational Definition."
4. Compare the suggestions of Dan Ben-Amos, "Toward a Definition of Folklore in Context," esp. 13.
5. See the excellent discussion by Pamela Milne, "Folktales and Fairy Tales: An Evaluation of Two Proppian Analyses of Biblical Narrative."
6. For an overview of the current debate, see Dan Ben-Amos, *Folklore Genres,* and the articles in Alan Dundes, ed., *The Study of Folklore,* 4–51.
7. F. J. Child's *English and Scottish Popular Ballads* remains the most important collection of English and Scottish ballads. Ballads have been recovered from old manuscripts, daybooks, family lists, and broadsides, some centuries old, the oldest known balladlike work being in a thirteenth-century manuscript. Since the eighteenth century, ballads also have been collected directly from oral tradition. MacEdward Leach, *The Ballad Book,* 34–36.

   The Milman Parry Collection is a collection of over 12,500 texts, some on more than 3,500 phonograph discs, others in dictation. The texts include epic and lyric songs and conversations with singers collected by Parry in Yugoslavia in 1934 and 1935. It is from this collection that Lord draws the material to be compared with Homeric epic. The collection is currently housed in the Harvard Center for the Study of Oral Literature, Cambridge, Massachusetts.
8. See Ben-Amos, "Toward a Definition," 9.
9. Toelken, *Dynamics,* 38.
10. On the formula, see Lord, *Singer,* 30–67.
11. See the fine study of design patterns in southwestern Nigerian *adire* cloths by S. P. X. Battestini, *"Sémiotique de l'adire."*
12. These foci of interest are found in David E. Bynum's *The Daemon in the Wood.*

Chapter 1

1. On "texture," see Alan Dundes, *Interpreting Folklore,* 22–23; Dan Ben-Amos, "Toward a Definition of Folklore in Context," 11. Jason and Segal divide

further between the levels of wording and poetic texture and suggest layers within each of these. See *Patterns in Oral Literature,* 3.

2. On the text, see Ben-Amos, "Toward a Definition," 10; Dundes, *Interpreting Folklore,* 23; Jason and Segal, *Patterns,* 3.

3. The Type Index is Stith Thompson's translation and enlargement of Antti Aarne's *Verzeichnis der Märchentypen.* (*The Types of the Folktale*). See also Thompson's *The Motif-Index of Folk-Literature.*

4. For a thorough discussion of the methodology and interests of the Historic-Geographic School, see Stith Thompson, *The Folktale;* for a classic application of the methodology, see Thompson's "The Star Husband Tale."

5. See the concise critique by Alan Dundes in *The Study of Folklore,* 415; and the comments of Roger D. Abrahams, "Personal Power and Social Restraint in the Definition of Folklore," 26.

6. Robert Dorson, *Folklore: Selected Essays,* 19–20.

7. For a well articulated antihistoricist position in the case of the "the Jacob conflict narratives," see Thomas L. Thompson, "Conflict of Themes in the Jacob Narrative." Donald Redford is generally extremely careful to reject historicism in his study of the Joseph tale (*A Study of the Biblical Story of Joseph, Genesis 37–50*), though even he may fall into the trap of dating via the typological in an attempt to date too precisely common literary motifs such as the reward to Joseph (ring, linen garments, and gold chain, 225–226) or the wrongfully accused wisdom hero who saves the land (241). Are the specifications of these motifs found in the Joseph tale so clearly Egyptian in provenance and second third of the first millennium B.C. in date? Contrast the approach of Hermann Gunkel, *Esther,* 41, 241n.

8. See Dorson, *Folklore: Selected Essays,* 199–222; Richard M. Dorson, ed., *Folklore and Traditional History;* Robert C. Culley, "Oral Tradition and Historicity"; Jan Vansina, *Oral Tradition: A Study in Historical Methodology;* Ruth Finnegan, "A Note on Oral Tradition and Historical Evidence"; A. B. Lord, "History and Tradition in Balkan Oral Epic and Ballad."

9. See Susan Niditch and Robert Doran, "The Success Story of the Wise Courtier" (on the end of "hand-writing-on-wall" episode in Daniel). David E. Bynum, *The Daemon in the Wood,* 78–79. See the criticism of historicism by Vladimir Propp, *Theory and History of Folklore,* 59–60, 87–88.

10. Dorothy Irvin, *Mytharion: The Comparison of Tales from the Old Testament and the Ancient Near East.*

11. Gunkel refers to the research of Aarne (p. 11) and frequently employs material from the Grimm collection and others to place Old Testament tales in a comparative context (see, for example, p. 125). The translation of this important work is long overdue but should be available soon from the Almond Press.

12. Niditch and Doran, ("The Success Story") also make use of Thompson's indices, as does David Gunn in "Traditional Narrative Composition in the 'Succession Narrative.' " Gunn points to recurring narrative patterns comparable to Robert Alter's "type scenes" (*The Art of Biblical Narrative,* 53–62) and places these in the context of traditional literature.

13. See the comments of Alan Dundes, *The Morphology of North American Indian Tales,* 53. See also the critique by Jay D. Edwards, *The Afro-American Trickster Tale: A Structural Analysis,* 24, n. 28.

14. For a bibliography of the work of Albert Bates Lord, see Edward R. Haymes, *A Bibliography of Studies Relating to Parry's and Lord's Oral Theory; John Miles Foley, Oral-Formulaic Theory and Research: An Introduction and Annotated Bibliography*, 399–414.

15. See S. Niditch, "The Composition of Isaiah 1." See also David Gunn, "Traditional Narrative"; and "Narrative Patterns and Oral Tradition in Judges and Samuel."

16. Bynum, *The Daemon*.

17. Bynum, *The Daemon*, 77–81. Hermann Gunkel shows sensitivity to the general and the specific folktale motifs (see *Das Märchen*, 11, 161).

18. V. Propp, *The Morphology of the Folktale* (published in Russian in 1928). See the important translation corrections provided by Heda Jason and Dimitri Segal in "The Problem of 'Tale Role' and 'Character' in Propp's Work," in *Patterns*, 313–20. For an introduction to the work of Lévi-Strauss, see his *Structural Anthropology*. For the approach of Algirdas Julian Greimas, who combines Proppian and Lévi-Straussian methodologies, see his *"Le conte populaire Russe (analyse fonctionnelle)"; Sémantique structurale;* "The Interpretation of Myth: Theory and Practice." For further bibliography and applications of structuralist methodologies, see Jason and Segal, *Patterns; Elli Köngäs Maranda and Pierre Maranda, Structural Models in Folklore and Transformational Essays*.

   Structuralist criticism of the Bible has become a significant field in its own right. See Robert M. Polzin, *Biblical Structuralism: Method and Subjectivity in the Study of Ancient Texts;* Roland Barthes et al., *Structural Analysis and Biblical Exegesis*, and its excellent bibliography, 110–65; David Jobling, *The Sense of Biblical Narrative: Three Structural Analyses in the Old Testament;* Daniel Patte, ed., *Genesis 2 and 3: Kaleidoscopic Structural Readings*.

19. Alan Dundes, "From Etic to Emic Units in the Structural Study of Folktales." See also his *Morphology*, 59; Kenneth L. Pike, *Language in Relation to a Unified Theory of the Structure of Behavior*, 75.

20. Propp, *Morphology*, 43.

21. Propp, *Morphology*, 21–22. See also the lengthier discussion in Propp, *Theory and History*, 82–99 (a translation of an essay originally published in 1928).

22. Alan Dundes, "From Etic to Emic"; see also Heda Jason, "A Model for Narrative Structure in Oral Literature," in Jason and Segal, *Patterns*, 99–139, esp. 106–7.

23. See Alan Dundes's discussion in *Interpreting Folklore*, 35.

24. Propp, *Theory and History*, 11, 50, 110, 115.

25. Compare Bynum's use of motif, and see Heda Jason's discussion of Propp (Bynum, *The Daemon*, 77–81; Jason and Segal, *Patterns*, 3; Jason, "A Model," 116).

26. See Propp, *Theory and History*, 82–99, also found in French, *"Les Transformations des Contes Merveilleux,"* translated in Tzvetan Todorov, *Théorie de la littérature*, 234–62. Compare Bynum, *The Daemon*, 77–81; Alan Dundes, "The Making and Breaking of a Friendship as a Structural Frame in African Folk Tales"; and Jason, "A Model, esp. 106–12.

27. See the critical yet sympathetic analyses of Propp's work by Max Lüthi,

The European Folktale: Form and Nature, 128–29; A. Liberman's Introduction in Propp, *Theory and History,* xxxi–xxxii.

28. J. M. Sasson, *Ruth: A Translation with a Philological Commentary and a Formalist-Folklorist Interpretation.*

29. See, for example, Robert Culley, "Themes and Variations in Three Groups of Old Testament Narratives"; *Studies in the Structure of Hebrew Narrative;* "Punishment Stories in the Legends of the Prophets."

30. Dan Ben-Amos, "Narrative Forms in the Haggadah: Structural Analysis," Ph.D. diss., Indiana University, 1966. Dundes, *Morphology;* "Structural Typology in North American Indian Folktales." Note also the morphological approach to riddles by Robert A. Georges and Alan Dundes, "Toward a Structural Definition of the Riddle"; and to proverbs by Alan Dundes, "On the Structure of the Proverb." See also Carole R. Fontaine, *Traditional Sayings in the Old Testament,* 34–38, 164–66.

31. André Jolles, *Einfache Formen.*

32. Claus Westermann, *The Promises to the Fathers,* 31–35; see the critique by John Van Seters, *Abraham in History and Tradition,* 134–38.

33. Carl Wilhelm von Sydow, *"Kategorien der Prosa-Volksdichtung";* "Popular Prose Traditions and Their Classification."

34. Albert de Pury, *Promesse divine et légende cultuelle dans le cycle de Jacob,* 2 vols.

35. Lüthi, *European Folktale,* (originally published in 1947). See also his "Aspects of the *Märchen* and the Legend."

36. William McKane, *Studies in the Patriarchal Narratives,* 16.

37. De Pury, *Promesse Divine,* 478–83.

38. Lüthi, *European Folktale,* 3.

39. See Dan Ben-Amos, "Analytical Categories and Ethnic Genres," 215. See also his comments on the essay by Burke Long in *Semeia* 3, 131. Though his own approach to genre is itself rather loose, Carl A. Keller does point to some of the inadequacies of describing Israelite literature in terms of European genres (*"Die Gefährdung der Anfrau."*)

40. Dan Ben-Amos, "Narrative Forms in the Haggadah: Structural Analysis," 72–74.

41. See Alan Dundes's comments on myth and folktale in *Morphology,* 110–11. See also Liberman's introduction in V. Propp, *Theory and History,* xxviii.

42. J. G. von Hahn, *Sagwissenschaftliche Studien;* Otto Rank, "The Myth of the Birth of the Hero," originally published in 1914; Lord Raglan, *The Hero* (originally published in 1936). See Joseph Campbell, *The Hero with a Thousand Faces;* and the discussions by Richard M. Dorson, ed., *Folklore and Folklife,* 34; and Alan Dundes, *Analytical Essays,* 151–62.)

43. Dundes, *Interpreting Folklore,* 223–61, esp. 232–33.

44. Ronald Hendel, "The Epic of the Patriarch: The Jacob Cycle and the Narrative Traditions of Canaan and Israel."

45. Axel Olrik, "Epic Laws of Folk Narrative."

46. See Hermann Gunkel, *Legends,* 40–58 (first published in 1901).

47. Van Seters, *Abraham,* 167–71, 183.

48. For a fine contrast between Propp and Lévi-Strauss, see David Pace, "Beyond Morphology: Lévi-Strauss and the Analysis of Folktales." Also see the discussion by A. Liberman, introduction, in V. Propp, *Theory and His-*

tory, xxxii–xliv. This volume also provides a reprint of Lévi-Strauss's critique of Propp originally published in Lévi-Strauss, *Structural Anthropology*, and Propp's rejoinder (67–81).

49. See the questions raised by Alan Dundes, *Interpreting Folklore*, 35–36 and Richard Dorson, ed., *Folklore and Folklife*, 35–36.

50. For an interesting critique of Lévi-Strauss, see Morris Freilich, "Lévi-Strauss' Myth of Method." See also the article by Robert Culley, "Structural Analysis: Is It Done with Mirrors?"

51. So Lévi-Strauss, "The Structural Study of Myth."

52. Edmond Leach, *Genesis As Myth and other Essays*, 7–23; see the critique by J. A. Emerton, "An Examination of a Recent Structuralist Interpretation of Genesis XXXVIII."

53. Robert Oden, "Transformations in Near Eastern Myths"; "Divine Aspirations in Atrahasis and in Genesis 1–11"; Robert M. Polzin, *Biblical Structuralism*.

54. Leach, *Genesis As Myth*, 7–8.

55. Udo Strutynski, "The Survival of Indo-European Mythology in Germanic Legendry."

56. Jan Vansina, *Oral Tradition: A Study in Historical Methodology;* and Walter Anderson, *Kaiser und Abt: Die Geschichte eines Schwankes*. See the critique of Anderson's well-known "law of self-correction" by Linda Degh and Andrew Vazsonyi, "The Hypothesis of Multi-Conduit Transmission in Folklore."

57. Hermann Gunkel evokes an all-too-romantic and idealized portrait of the professional storyteller poetically entertaining his simple shepherd audience (see *Legends*, 99; *Das Märchen*, 1–12; and the critique by Ronald Hendel, "The Epic of the Patriarch," 7–16). Yet allowing for certain dated assumptions, Gunkel's image is perferable to Donald Redford's "modern" suggestion that an author of "a Judah version/expansion" of the Joseph tale has rewritten, quoting and adapting, an earlier version of the tale, "the Reuben version" (*A Study*). Redford writes of the "creation" and "publication" of the tale, originally a *Märchen* (178–79). He writes of the writer of the Judah-expansion collecting tales about Jacob's sons (179) and of a still later Genesis editor, "A composer loath to reject anything short of gross theological error" (180). The image of a set "published text," neatly laid out before a series of expanders and editors in their scriptoria predominates.

58. Propp, *Theory and History*, 115.

59. See the summary of a paper recently delivered by Dan Ben-Amos (Program and Abstracts of the 1985 Meeting of the American Folklore Society). In this spirit are the first two chapters of Werner H. Kelber, *The Oral and the Written Gospel;* and the discussions of Robert Coote, "The Application of Oral Theory to Biblical Hebrew Literature," esp. 60–61; and Robert C. Culley, "Oral Tradition and the OT: Some Recent Discussion," 21.

60. Gunn, "Narrative Patterns and Oral Tradition."

61. See Lord, *Singer*, 13–29.

62. Dennis R. MacDonald, *The Legend and the Apostle: The Battle for Paul in Story and Canon;* see also Robert G. Boling, *Judges*, 31–35; E. F. Campbell, Jr., *Ruth*, 18–23.

63. William Whallon, *Formula, Character, and Context*; Robert Culley, *Oral Formulaic Language in the Biblical Psalms*; John Kselman, "The Recovery of Poetic Fragments from the Pentateuchal Priestly Source"; William J. Urbrock, "Evidences of Oral-Formulaic Composition in the Poetry of Job." See also Perry Bruce Yoder, "A-B Pairs and Oral Composition in Hebrew Poetry."

64. See Robert Coote, "Tradition, Oral, OT"; and "The Application"; S. Niditch, "The Composition of Isaiah 1," 518–520; Robert C. Culley, *Oral Formulaic Language*.

65. Robert Lowth, "Lecture XIX" Stanley Gevirtz, *Patterns in the Early Poetry of Israel*.

66. Robert C. Culley, ed., *Oral Tradition and Old Testament Studies Semeia* 5 (1976).

67. See Robert Coote, "The Application," 57; and Robert C. Culley, "The Oral Tradition and OT: Some Recent Discussion," 21.

68. Culley, "Oral Tradition," 19. See James A. Kugel, *The Idea of Biblical Poetry: Parallelism and Its History*, 76–87.

69. Susan Wittig, "Theories of Formulaic Narrative," 78–83.

70. Hymes, "Breakthrough into Performance."

71. See Irvin, *Mytharion*, 112–14.

72. See the article by Ilhan Basgoz, "The Tale-Singer and His Audience."

73. See Degh and Vazsonyi, "The Hypothesis of Multi-Conduit Transmission in Folklore," 241–52.

74. On performance context, see Barbara Kirshenblatt-Gimblett, "A Parable in Context: A Social Interactional Analysis of Storytelling Performance"; Herminia Q. Merez, "Filipino-American Erotica and the Ethnography of a Folkloric Event."

75. See Roger A. Abrahams, "Personal Power and Social Restraint in the Definition of Folklore," 24. See the critique of the Herder and Gunkel models by Ronald Hendel, "The Epic," 4, 10, 15.

76. Dan Ben-Amos, "Toward a Definition of Folklore in Context."

77. Robert R. Wilson, *Prophecy and Society of Ancient Israel*; and *Genealogy and History in the Biblical World*. See also Robert Culley and Thomas W. Overholt, eds. *Anthropological Perspectives on Old Testament Prophecy*; Burke O. Long, "The Social Function of Conflict Among the Prophets"; Susan Niditch, "The Visionary"; and *Chaos to Cosmos: Studies in Biblical Patterns of Creation*. The latter was influenced by theoretical approaches developed by Clifford Geertz, Victor Turner, and Mary Douglas, whose works include the following: Clifford Geertz, *The Interpretation of Cultures*; Victor Turner, *The Ritual Process*; Mary Douglas, *Purity and Danger*.

78. See, for example, W. H. R. Rivers's 1912 article, "The Sociological Significance of Myth"; and the critique of functionalism by Roger D. Abrahams, "Personal Power and Social Restraint in the Definition of Folklore," 26–27; and by Richard M. Dorson, ed., *Folklore and Folklife*, 20–25.

79. Clifford Geertz, "Religion as a Cultural System."

80. David Bynum, for example, deals not with "myths," "legends," and "folktales" but with "oral narrative," a heading under which all fall (*The Daemon*).

81. Victor Turner, *Dramas, Fields, and Metaphors: Symbolic Action in Human Society*.

82. Abrahams, "Personal Power," 26–27.
83. For two fine essays that ask some of these questions, see Barbara Kirshenblatt-Gimblett's "Culture Shock and Narrative Creativity"; and "A Parable in Context: A Social Interactional Analysis of Storytelling Performance."
84. George Mendenhall, *The Tenth Generation*; Norman Gottwald, *The Tribes of Yahweh: A Sociology of the Religion of Liberated Israel 1250–1050 B.C.*
85. Paredes and Bauman, eds. *Toward New Perspectives in Folklore* (Austin: University of Texas Press, 1972), 16–30.
86. Paredes and Bauman, *Toward New Perspectives*, 31–41.
87. See, for example, the abstract of Rita Ross, "The Forbidden Chamber."
88. See, for example, Vera Mark, "Images of Women in Gascon Verbal Art."
89. See, for example, Pamela Wilson, "Keeping the Record Straight: The Social Functions of Gossip."
90. See Margaret Mills, "Afghan Popular Romances and Creative Consciousness."
91. See Pamela Wilson, "Keeping the Record Straight."
92. See the abstract of a paper by Torborg Lundell, "Making Mother Conform to Standards."
93. See Alan Dundes's *Analytic Essays*, 14–16; and *Interpreting Folklore*, 33–61. Dundes also makes some interesting points about the psychology of collecting folklore. The collections we have reflect the collectors, not always the culture (*Analytic Essays*, 121–29). Other applications of psychoanalytical approach are Dundes's " 'To Love My Father All': A Psychoanalytic Study of the Folktale Source of *King Lear*"; and Ben Rubenstein, "The Meaning of the Cinderella Story in the Development of a Little Girl."
94. See the discussion by Richard M. Dorson, ed., *Folklore and Folklife*, 25–33.
95. Otto Rank, *The Myth of the Birth of the Hero and Other Writings*.
96. Joseph Campbell, *The Hero with a Thousand Faces*; Erich Neumann, *The Origins and History of Consciousness*. See also Carlos C. Drake, "Jung and His Critics"; and "Jungian Psychology and Its Use in Folklore."

Chapter 2

1. Gerhard von Rad assigns 12:10–20 to the Yahwist and 20 to the Elohist, and is noncommittal about 26:1–22 (*Genesis*, 162–64, 221, 266). E. A. Speiser assigns 12:10–20 and 26:1–22 to J, 20 to E (*Genesis*). Klaus Koch considers J and E to be redactors of 12:10–20 and 20, respectively, and J or "a second J source" to have redacted 26:1–22 (*The Growth of the Biblical Tradition*, 129–30). Gunkel assigns 12:10–20 to "J", 20:10–20 to E, and the account in Genesis 26 to "J^R." For his relative chronology for the three, see *Genesis*, 225–26.
2. Koch, *Growth*, 122. For suggestions that Genesis 26 provides the more "original" version, see E. Maly, "Genesis 12,10–20; 20,1–18; 26,7–11 and the Penteteuchal Question."
3. Westermann, *The Promises to the Fathers*, 32–35; Koch, *Growth*, 120.
4. John Van Seters, *Abraham in History and Tradition*, 134–38.

5. Koch, *Growth*, 127.
6. Gunkel, *Legends*, 24–27
7. Gunkel, *Legends*, 47.
8. Gunkel, *Legends*, 1–5, 18–19, 40–41, 128–30.
9. Gunkel, *Legends*, 39–41, 67, 82–85, 99.
10. Gunkel, *Genesis* 225–26; and Van Seters, *Abraham*, 183.
11. Samuel, "The Haggada with Scripture."
12. Robert Polzin, "The Ancesters of Israel in Danger."
13. Robert Alter, *The Art of Biblical Narrative*.
14. James G. Williams, "The Beautiful and the Barren: Conventions in Biblical Type-Scenes."
15. Robert Culley, *Studies in the Structure of Hebrew Narrative*.
16. D. Hans Schmidt and Paul Kahle, *Volkserzählungen aus Palästina*, 2 vols., vol. 1, 45–53, no. 24; Van Seters, *Abraham*, 168n. See also Culley's list of tales, including Gen. 12:10–20, which trace a pattern he describes as problem/deception/solution. This pattern begins to anticipate some of our work here ("Themes and Variations in Three Groups of OT Narratives," esp. 5). See also his "Structuralism," 173–74.
17. Robert Polzin, *Biblical Structuralism: Method and Subjectivity in the Study of Ancient Texts*, 10–11. For some interesting but brief comments on the various levels of structure, see Culley, "Structural Analysis," 170–72.
18. See, for example, A Julien Greimas, "The Interpretation of Myth: Theory and Practice," 97; Jay D. Edwards, *The Afro-American Trickster Tale: A Structural Analysis*, 88, n. 59.
19. The specific elements of content are somewhat similar to the "motifemes" by which Alan Dundes and Dan Ben-Amos define folktale morphologies, though further gradations may be suggested between Dundes's "emic" and "etic." See Alan Dundes, *The Morphology of North American Indian Folktales*; and Dan Ben-Amos, "Narrative Forms in the Haggadah: Structural Analysis."
20. The Greek text (G) provides some variant readings, but the Masoretic text (MT) is preferable or equally desirable in these cases. At 12:13, whereas the MT has the second person, "You are my sister," G allows for a quotation, "I am his sister." Either reading is acceptable. At 12:17, G provides a longer variant in describing the plagues. At 12:19 MT provides the slightly shorter reading, and G has "and now here is your wife *before you.*" At 12:20 G contains a transitional addition, "and Lot was with him" (cf. 12:4).
21. A. B. Lord, *The Singer of Tales*, 53.
22. Gunkel, *Legends*, 71.
23. The Hebrew Masoretic text (MT) of v. 4 makes little sense. The translation suggests the emended text, *hăgam ṣaddîq tahărōg,* "Would you kill even a righteous man?"
    In v. 16 MT has *w,* "and," before "justified." The above translation suggests its omission.
24. Gunkel points to this contrast, *Legends*, 82–83.
25. See Albright's introduction to Gunkel's *Legends*, ix.
26. Gunkel *Legends*, 124–25.
27. On Grimm Brothers' alteration of original texts, see T. Lundell, "Making Mother Conform to Standards."

28. Van Seters, *Abraham*, 177–83.
29. Van Seter's translation makes the two phrases in 20:11 and 26:9 seem more alike than they are (*Abraham*, 180).
30. Axel Olrik, "Epic Laws of Folk Narrative."
31. Recall the discussion of Degh and Vazsonyi, "The Hypothesis," in Dan Ben-Amos and Kenneth S. Goldstein, eds., *Folklore: Performance and Communication*, 207–52.
32. See Vladimir Propp, *The Morphology of the Folktale*, 35 ff.
33. Robert Pelton, *The Trickster in West Africa*, 6–7; Daniel Brinton, *The Myths of the New World*, 161–62.
34. Mac Linscott Ricketts, "The North American Indian Trickster," 336.
35. Mac Linscott Ricketts, "The Structure and Religious Significance of the Trickster–Transformer–Culture Hero in the Mythology of the North American Indians," 589.
36. Paul Radin, *The Trickster*, 133, 136–37.
37. Paul Radin, "The Religion of the North American Indians," 354–55, 359–60.
38. Pelton, *Trickster*, 14.
39. Alan Dundes points to a Trickster morphology common in North American Indian tales. His motifemic outline for these tales is "Lack/Deceit/Deception/Lack Liquidated," (*Morphology*, 72). In a later work, Dundes outlines a "structural frame" particularly common in African tales: Friendship, Contract, Violation (e.g., by means of deceit), Discovery (of Violation), End of Friendship ("The Making and Breaking of Friendship as a Structural Frame in African Folk Tales.") Dundes's "structural frame" touches a level of description somewhere between our "specific" and "typological." For other work with trickster patterns, see Edwards, *Afro-American Trickster*, 18–65.
40. See Radin, *The Trickster*, 22–24. The version of the cycle provided by Radin is a translation of the performance by an elderly Winnebago Indian who lived near Winnebago, Nebraska, recorded in 1912 by Sam Blowsnake, Radin's informant (111, 4–60).
41. Radin, *The Trickster*, 102.
42. Dundes, *Morphology*, 104–5, 110.
43. References to many Norwegian examples of Type 1542 are found in R. Th. Christiansen, *Norske Eventyr*, 135–36. An English summary of *Norske Eventyr* is available in FFC 46 and is employed here.
44. Sandmel, "*Haggada*."
45. See also E. E. Evans-Pritchard, *The Zande Trickster*, 30.
46. Edwards, *Afro-American Trickster*, 72–73.
47. Edwards, *Afro-American Trickster*, 73.
48. So Gunkel's notion of the Yahwist's collection of sources (*Legends*, 124–25).
49. Speiser, *Genesis*, 91–94; "The Wife-Sister Motif in the Patriarchal Narratives"; See the criticism by Van Seters, *Abraham*, 74–75; and S. Greengus, "Sisterhood Adoption at Nuzi and the 'Wife-Sister' in Genesis."
50. See Thompson type 1542 for examples.
51. Williams, "The Beautiful," 112, 116–77.
52. Martin Noth, *A History of Pentateuchal Traditions* (Englewood Cliffs, NJ: Prentice-Hall, 1972), 102–07.

53. See A. Leo Oppenheim, *The Interpretation of Dreams in the Ancient Near East;* Susan Niditch, *The Symbolic Vision in Biblical Tradition.*
54. The tales in Genesis 26 are a young man's tales too quickly followed by the story of the old man in chapter 27. Were Genesis 26 to come earlier in the Isaac narrative it would hold a place comparable to Genesis 12 in the tales of Abraham. See also Gunkel's comments (*Genesis*, 299).
55. Koch, *Growth*, 122.
56. See Gunkel, *Genesis*, 225–26; Van Seters, *Abraham*, 183.
57. On the place of Genesis 26 in the structure of Genesis, see Michael Fishbane, *Text and Texture*, 42, 46–47; J. P. Fokkelman, *Narrative Art in Genesis*, 113–15.
58. Robert Polzin, "Ancestress."

Chapter 3

1. Joseph Blenkinsopp begins to explore the relationship between biography as a genre, the folktale, and biblical narrative in "Biographic Patterns in Biblical Narrative." His concluding suggestion concerning the relationship between the folktale pattern and initiation is one long emphasized by others (see below). For a more systematic study of biography in late antiquity, see Patricia Cox, *Biography in Late Antiquity: A Quest for the Holy Man;* see also Arnaldo Momigliano, *The Development of Greek Biography.*
2. For a discussion of the bildungsroman in British literature, see Jerome H. Buckley, *Season of Youth: The Bildungsroman from Dickens to Golding;* for a discussion of the genre and classic German examples, see Martin Swales, *The German Bildungsroman from Wieland to Hesse;* Rolf Selbman, *Der deutsche Bildungsroman.*
3. See the review of works on the hero pattern by Alan Dundes, "The Hero Pattern and the Life of Jesus," 223–32, and chap. 1, n. 49. For a more specialized study of the pattern of "plot-motifs" and "traditional episodes" (Irvin's terms) in Joseph and Moses narratives, see D. Irvin, "The Joseph and Moses Stories as Narrative in the Light of Ancient Near Eastern Narrative."
4. Lord Raglan, *The Hero*, 1–16 and throughout. On history and folklore, see chap. 1, n. 16.
5. Otto Rank, "The Myth of the Birth of Hero," 71–72, 84–85, 91.
6. See Philip Freund's introduction to Rank's *The Myth*, vii–ix.
7. Dundes's definition certainly has its own problems (see "The Hero Pattern," 224, and the introduction to a more recent work edited by him, *Sacred Narrative*, 1).
8. See the critique by Dundes, "The Hero Pattern," 232, 234, and on the larger issue of cross-cultural comparison, see V. Cook, "Lord Raglan's Hero—A Cross Cultural Critique."
9. See also Thompson type 725. In a brief study, Peter Miscall points to the pattern of treachery between brothers, separation, and reunion found in Jacob and Joseph narratives ("The Jacob and Joseph Stories as Analogies"). See also Thomas Thompson's discussion of recurring themes of "the un-

promising son" and the conflict between brothers in tales of Jacob ("Conflict of Themes in the Jacob Narrative").

10. Dundes, "The Hero Pattern," 232–33.
11. A. B. Lord, "The Gospels as Oral Traditional Literature," 39.
12. Rank, "The Hero" 19, 30, 256.
13. See the discussion in S. Niditch, *Chaos to Cosmos: Studies in Biblical Patterns of Creation*, 45–50.
14. A. B. Lord, *The Singer of Tales*, 100–138; David E. Bynum, "Themes of the Young Hero in Serbocroatian Oral Epic Tradition."
15. Bynum, "Themes," 1302.
16. Bynum, "Themes," 1302.
17. Hermann Gunkel, *Legends of Genesis*, 48–87; *Genesis*, introduction, li–lv; "Jakob"; "Die Komposition der Joseph-Geschichten."
18. Gunkel, *Legends*, 79–80, *Genesis*, 292.
19. Gunkel, *Legends*, 81. See also in "Jakob," 343.
20. Gunkel, *Genesis*, xlvi; *Legends*, 58 ff. See William McKane, 28–36.
21. See comments of McKane, *Studies*, 36.
22. Gunkel, *Legends*, 82–84.
23. Gunkel, *Genesis*, 398: "*zarten und ruhrenden.*"
24. McKane, *Studies*, 37; Gunkel, *Genesis*, intro. xxxiv: "*eine reifer gewordene ästhetische Empfindung*"; "Die Komposition," 59–67; *Das Märchen*, 163.
25. Gunkel, *Legends*, 84; *Genesis*, intro. iv: "*schleppend.*"
26. Redford, *A Study*, 68, 68 ff., 72 f., 77.
27. Redford, *A Study*, 156–58.
28. Redford, *A Study*, 149–50.
29. Redford, *A Study*, 140–43, 152–58.
30. Redford, *A Study*, 28–65.
31. I translate *tām*, ("complete, finished") as "acculturated" to contrast Jacob's polish with Esau's roughness and to evoke the nature/culture contrast in characterizations of the boys (a dichotomy emphasized by Ronald Hendel, "The Epic of the Patriarch: The Jacob Cycle and the Narrative Traditions of Canaan and Israel," 152–57); I overliteralize *kî ṣayid bĕpîw* ("because he supplied his appetite for game") to capture the cadences of the Hebrew. Compare translations by Robert Alter, *The Art of Biblical Narrative*, 42; and Michael Fishbane, *Text and Texture*, 44.
32. James A. Kugel, *The Idea of Biblical Poetry: Parallelism and Its History*. Note Kugel's comments on "terseness" as "a variously manifested standard" (87–88).
33. Chaps. 39–41 in places may evidence somewhat longer phrasing, but not consistently or dominantly enough to diverge from the Joseph narrative as a whole.
34. See the careful analyses of "brother" language by Fishbane, *Text and Texture*, 51, and of "elder/younger" language by J. P. Fokkelman, *Narrative Art in Genesis*, 106–7.
35. Susan Niditch, *The Symbolic Vision in Biblical Tradition*, 18–19; Niditch and Doran, "The Success Story."
36. Niditch and Doran, "The Success Story."
37. See Redford's comments. *A Study*, 87.
38. Redford distinguishes between recapitulation and embellishment (*A Study*,

76 ff.) and draws a further line between the good, controlled recapitulation of the Reuben version and a less appealing, verbose embellishment in the Judah version and chapter 39 (*A Study*, 77 ff.). I consider these forms of repetition to be of a piece throughout the tale.

39. See other examples in Redford, *A Study*, 77–85.
40. See Gunkel, *Legends*, 84.
41. On "wisdom" and speeches in the Joseph narrative, see G. von Rad, *Die Josephsgeschichte*, 13.

Chapter 4

1. On the annunciation, see Alter, *The Art of Biblical Narrative*, 82; and Michael Fishbane, *Text and Texture*, 59.
2. Warren S. Walker and Ahmet E. Uysal, *Tales Alive in Turkey*, 34–54. This tale was collected from Mehmet Anli, a prisoner in Senop Penitentiary.
3. A. B. Lord discussed Jacob and unusual birth in a Willis Wood lecture at Amherst College in October 1983; see also Ronald Hendel, "The Epic of the Patriarch: The Jacob Cycle and the Narrative Traditions of Canaan and Israel," 49–74; Fishbane, *Text and Texture*, 58; and Hermann Gunkel, *Genesis*, 182, 268.
4. See Hendel, "The Epic" 47–48, on *wayye'tar* ("he prayed").
5. Alter, *The Art*, 53–62.
6. So Fishbane, *Text and Texture*, 45; J. P. Fokkelman, *Narrative Art in Genesis*, 88–89.
7. So Fokkelman, *Narrative Art*, 90–91, and others.
8. On women and ambiguity in Israelite and classical Jewish literature, see Susan Niditch, "The Wronged Woman Righted: An Analysis of Genesis 38"; *Chaos to Cosmos*, 36–37; J. R. Baskin, "The Separation of Women in Rabbinic Judaism."
9. See Niditch, "The Wronged Woman," 144–46.
10. Compare Robert Alter's reading of this scene in *The Art*, 186–88.
11. Interesting comparative material on the association of women with the private rather than public realm is provided by Elizabeth Stern, "Shameful Sorcery in Old Norse Tradition," a paper delivered at the October 1985 meeting of the American Folklore Society, Cincinnati, Ohio.
12. See Fishbane on Jacob as "hireling," *Text and Texture*, 57.
13. See Niditch, *Chaos to Cosmos*, 17–18, 45–50.
14. Otto Rank, "The Myth of the Birth of the Hero."
15. See motifs P230.1; P233.4
16. See chap. 3, n. 34, and Hendel, "The Epic," 152–57.
17. Hendel, "The Epic," 152–57; see also Gunkel, *Genesis*, 298.
18. Donald Redford, *A Study of the Biblical Story of Joseph, Genesis 37–50*, 104. See also George W. Coats, *From Canaan to Egypt: Structural and Theological Context for the Joseph Story*, 82.
19. See A. Leo Oppenheim, *The Interpretation of Dreams in the Ancient Near East*, 208.
20. Note that Judah and Reuben are not portrayed heroically in the capture

and selling of Joseph. Reuben takes his eyes off the boy. Judah is an un-caring sneak, who sells the boy without a second thought. This portrayal of Judah is consistent with later images of the lout, who would, with a phrase, throw his daughter-in-law into the flames (Gen. 38:24). Compare Redford's treatment (*A Study*, 139–43).

21. In Walker and Uysal, *Tales*, 10–24.

22. In *Chaos to Cosmos*, with an approach influenced by the work of Eliade, van Gennep, and Turner, I have explored the boundary where literary patterns meet ritual patterns.

23. On Jacob's marriage in the light of kinship studies, see Robert Oden, "Jacob as Father, Husband, and Nephew: Kinship Studies and the Patriarchal Narratives."

24. Mircea Eliade, *Shamanism*.

25. For a quite different interpretation of God's role in Jacob and Joseph narratives, see Peter Miscall, "The Jacob and Joseph Stories as Analogies," 33–34.

26. See Susan Niditch, *The Symbolic Vision in Biblical Tradition*, 1–19.

27. Alter, *The Art*, 53–63; also James G. Williams, "The Beautiful and the Barren: Conventions in Biblical Type-Scenes."

28. Hendel, "The Epic," 181–82.

29. See Niditch, "The Wronged Woman."

30. Compare Fishbane's outline in *Text and Texture*, 42.

31. On relationships and trickery in cross-cousin marriage, see Oden, "Jacob as Father," 199–202.

32. Redford, *A Study*, 93; see also Dorothy Irvin, "The Joseph and Moses Stories as Narrative in the Light of Ancient Near Eastern Narrative," 185–88.

33. See Eliade, *Shamanism*, 71–81.

34. Gerhard von Rad, "The Joseph Narrative and Ancient Wisdom," 292–300, esp. 295; Gunkel, *Genesis*, 431.

35. On the significance of these gods and their ancient Near Eastern context, see Hendel, "The Epic," 113 and n. 27.

36. On Rachel's deception in the context of other ancient Near Eastern literature, see Handel, "The Epic," 112–16. Correspondence between Rachel's deception and Jacob's have been explored thoroughly by Fokkelman, *Narrative Art*, 170, 139–41; and Fishbane, *Text and Texture*, 41.

37. See the review and discussion by Hendel, "The Epic," 122–29.

38. On resonances of the new name *Yiśrā'ēl* and the significance of the folk etymology, see Fokkelman, *Narrative Art*, 216–17.

39. For one reading of symmetries in the Jacob narrative that nicely emphasizes the reversal in chap. 33, see Fishbane, *Text and Texture*, 42, 52.

40. Jeffrey Tigay suggests that this ending was not a part of the earlier Old Babylonian version of the epic (*The Evolution of the Gilgamesh Epic*, 143, 146–49).

41. On the place of Genesis 34 and 35 in the current composition, see Fishbane, *Text and Texture*, 46–47.

42. Peter Miscall views the scenes of reconciliation in Jacob and Joseph tales as indicators of the character development of each hero and as comments on the role of God in the lives of human beings ("The Jacob and Joseph Stories," 36–39).

43. Redford, *A Study*, 104; Coats, *From Canaan*, 86–87.
44. So too T. Thompson and D. Irvin, "The Joseph and Moses Narratives," in J. Hayes and J. M. Miller, *Israelite and Judaean History (Philadelphia: Westminster, 1977)*, 179.
45. Shemaryahu Talmon, "Wisdom in the Book of Esther"; Gerhard von Rad, "The Joseph Narrative and Ancient Wisdom."
46. Chapter 49 presents a scene as much associated with the death of the hero in Israelite tradition as is the annunciation with his birth. This testament of the patriarch signals the transition from life to death and, with this passage, the acquisition of the special numinous status of the nearly dead.
47. See the discussion by Redford, *A Study*, 238–43.

Chapter 5

1. E.g., Shemaryahu Talmon, "Wisdom in the Book of Esther," 455.
2. Talmon, "Wisdom," 454–55; L. A. Rosenthal, *"Die Josephsgeschichte mit den Buchem Ester und Daniel verglichen"; "Nochmals der Vergleich Ester-Joseph"*; M. Gan, "The Book of Esther in the Light of Joseph's Fate in Egypt. So also Arndt Meinhold, *"Die Gattung der Josephsgeschichte und des Esterbuches: Diasporanovelle II,"* 75. Sandra Beth Berg agrees in a nuanced way with dependence theories. See her careful discussion in *The Book of Esther: Motifs, Themes and Structure*, 123–43.
3. Meinhold, *"Die Gattung"* I, II.
4. Berg, *Book of Esther*, 135–36 and 157–58, n. 52.
5. Meinhold, *"Die Gattung"* I, 316; *"Die Gattung"* II, 82, 84, 85.
6. See the chart in *"Die Gattung"* II, 88–89.
7. Berg, *Book of Esther*, 136.
8. Cf. similar findings in chapter 2 and in Susan Niditch and Robert Doran, "The Success Story of the Wise Courtier."
9. Gunkel points to qualities of "exaggeration" (*Esther*, 50) and the style of superlatives (*Esther*, 51) in Esther, suggesting parallels with Daniel, Judith, and 3 Macc.
10. The phrase "and the matter was good in the eyes of" (i.e., "it pleased") found at 1:21, 2:4, is found at Gen. 41:31. Deut. 1:23, Josh. 22:30; 22:33, 1 Kings 3:10 and elsewhere and is one of the examples of the boundary where idiomatic speech meets formulaic construction. In any event, this particular idiom is the preferred mode, in Esther, of expressing approval of a decision (see also 5:14).
11. Elias Bickerman, *Four Strange Books of the Bible*, 172–81.
12. Hans Bardtke, *Das Buch Esther*, 248–52.
13. On unified quality of Esther, see Bickerman, *Four Strange Books*, 172–81; Berg, *Book of Esther*, 31–35, 72.
14. Henri Cazelles, *"Notes sur la composition du rouleau d'Esther,"* 17–29, esp. 28; J. C. H. Lebram, *"Purimfest und Estherbuch"*; Claus Schedl, *"Das Buch Esther,"* 90.
15. See the Norwegian tale "The Old Woman Against the Stream," a tale col-

lected by Peter Christen Asbjørnsen, found in Peter Christen Asbjørnsen and Jørgen Moe, *Norwegian Folktales*, 112-14.

16. E.g., Mary Gendler, "The Restoration of Vashti," 241-47.
17. On old men and foolish kings, see Talmon, "Wisdom," 450-51.
18. Talmon, "Wisdom," 441-43.
19. Alan Dundes, *The Morphology of North American Indian Folktales*, 59, 80, 98.
20. W. Lee Humphreys, "A Life-style for Diaspora: A Study of the Tales of Esther and Daniel"; Meinhold, *"Die Gattung"* I and II; Talmon, "Wisdom."
21. Contra Meinhold, who emphasizes the importance of the hero's ethnic identity in Joseph (*"Die Gattung"* I, 311-13; II, 76-78.)
22. See George Mendenhall, *The Tenth Generation*, 122-41, esp. 136-41; Norman K. Gottwald, *The Tribes of Yahweh*, 213-19, 401-25.
23. See the Turkish tale "The Daughters of the Broom Thief," for a good example of this motif (Warren S. Walker and Ahmet E. Uysal, *Tales Alive in Turkey*, 135-39). For an example of the interceding queen, see "The Unjust King and the Wicked Goldsmith," in J. H. Knowles, *Folk-Tales of Kashmir*, 229-32. In this tale, the intercession of the good queen becomes a cause for her banishment, which in turn leads to other adventures. Work with the Motif Index instructs one about the stuff of traditional tales, the many combinations of motifs possible, the process of variation and multiformity that is traditional-style composition.
24. Berg emphasizes the theme of dual loyalty to state and people found in Esther (*Book of Esther*, 100). See also Meinhold, *"Die Gattung"* I, 319.
25. Robert Gordis, "Studies in the Esther Narrative," *JBL* 15 (1976):49-53.
26. For a striking example of this point of view, see Bernhard W. Anderson, "Esther," 828-30.
27. Gunkel, *Esther*, 1.
28. See Berg on themes of obedience and disobedience in Esther, which she sees as recurring and unifying in the work (*Book of Esther*, 72-82, 100).
29. See in this context Humphreys, "A Life-style," 223.
30. David Daube, *Collaboration with Tyranny in Rabbinic Law*. See also Moshe Greenberg, "Rabbinic Reflections on Defying Illegal Orders: Amasa, Abner, and Joab," 211-20.
31. See my review article, "Legends of Wise Heroes and Heroines," 445-46.
32. Theodor H. Gaster, *Purim and Hanukkah in Custom and Tradition*, 35; Bickerman, *Four Strange Books*, 199-200; Gunkel suggests that a more folkloristic work has been redacted by a later scholastic writer concerned with historical detail (*Esther*, 53-54).
33. Carey A. Moore, *Esther*, xli; Anderson, "Esther," 827-28.
34. A. Ungnad, *"Keilinschriftliche Beiträge zum Buch Ezra und Esther."* See also S. Horn, "Mordecai, A Historical Problem," 20-24.
35. Talmon, "Wisdom," 422.
36. Talmon, "Wisdom," 436.
37. See Gunkel, *Das Märchen im alten Testament*, 158, for some relevant observations.
38. Talmon, "Wisdom," 452-53.
39. Talmon, "Wisdom," 433.
40. Talmon, "Wisdom," 441, 452, 446.
41. Talmon, "Wisdom," 431, 433.

42. Axel Olrik, "Epic Laws of Folk Narrative"; Max Lüthi, *The European Folktale*, 56.
43. Meinhold, *"Die Gattung"* II, 92.
44. See Niditch, "Legends," 446.
45. See Niditch, "Legends," 446.
46. G. Gerleman, *Studien zu Esther; Stoff-Struktur-Stil-Sinn*, 10–28; *Esther*, 11–23.
47. Humphreys, "A Life-style"; Meinhold, *"Die Gattung"* I, II.
48. Samuel Sandmel, *The Hebrew Scriptures: An Introduction to Their Literature and Religious Ideas*, 450. See also Bruce W. Jones, "Two Misconceptions about the Book of Esther," 177.

Bibliography

Aarne, Antti. *Verzeichnis der Märchentypen.* FFC 3. Helsinki: Suomalainen tiedeakatemia, 1910.

Abrahams, Roger D. "Personal Power and Social Restraint in the Definition of Folklore." In *Toward New Perspectives in Folklore,* ed. Américo Paredes and Richard Bauman, 16–30. Austin: University of Texas, 1972.

Alter, Robert. *The Art of Biblical Narrative.* New York: Basic, 1981.

Anderson, Bernhard W. "Esther." IB vol. 3 (1954):823–74.

Anderson, Walter. *Kaiser und Abt: Die Geschichte eines Schwankes.* FFC 42. Helsinki: Suomalainen tiedeakatemia, 1923.

Asbjørnsen, Peter Christen, and Jørgen Moe. *Norwegian Folktales.* Trans. Pat Shaw Iversen and Carl Norman. New York: Viking, 1960.

Babcock-Abrahams, Barbara. " 'A Tolerated Margin of Mess': The Trickster and His Tales Reconsidered." *Journal of the Folklore Institute* 11 (1974):147–86.

Bardtke, Hans. *Das Buch Esther.* KAT 17/5. Gütersloh: Gerd Mohn, 1963.

Barthes, Roland, et al. *Structural Analysis and Biblical Exegesis.* Pittsburgh Theological Monograph Series. Pittsburgh: Pickwick, 1974.

Bascom, William R. "Verbal Art." *JAF* 68 (1955):245–52.

Basgoz, Ilhan. "The Tale-Singer and His Audience." In *Folklore: Performance and Communication,* 143–203. *See* Ben-Amos and Goldstein.

Baskin, J. R. "The Separation of Women in Rabbinic Judaism." In *Women, Religion and Social Change,* ed. Ellison B. Findly and Yvonne Y. Haddad, 3–18. Albany: State University of New York Press, 1985.

Battestini, S. P. X. *"Sémiotique de l'adire." Semiotica* 49 (1984):73–93.

Ben-Amos, Dan. "Analytical Categories and Ethnic Genres." In *Folklore Genres.*

———. "Narrative Forms in the Haggadah: Structural Analysis." Ph.D. diss., Indiana University, 1966.

_____. "Toward a Definition of Folklore in Context." In *Toward New Perspectives in Folklore*, 3–15. See Abrahams.

_____, ed. *Folklore Genres*. Publications of the American Folklore Society, Bibliographical and Special Series, vol. 26. Austin: University of Texas, 1976.

Ben-Amos, Dan, and Kenneth S. Goldstein, eds. *Folklore: Performance and Communication*. The Hague and Paris: Mouton, 1975.

Berg, Sandra Beth. *The Book of Esther: Motifs, Themes and Structures*. SBL Diss. Ser. 14. Missoula, MT: Scholars, 1979.

Bickerman, Elias. *Four Strange Books of the Bible*. New York: Schocken, 1967.

Blenkinsopp, Joseph. "Biographic Patterns in Biblical Narrative." *JSOT* 20 (1981):27–46.

Boling, Robert G. *Judges*. Anchor Bible. Garden City, NJ: Doubleday, 1975.

Brinton, Daniel. *The Myths of the New World*. New York: Leypoldt & Holt, 1968.

Buckley, Jerome H. *Season of Youth: The Bildungsroman from Dickens to Golding*. Cambridge: Harvard University Press, 1974.

Buss, Martin, J. "The Study of Forms." In *Old Testament Form Criticism*, ed. John H. Hayes, 1–56. San Antonio: Trinity University Press, 1974.

Bynum, David E. *The Daemon in the Wood*. Cambridge: Harvard Center for the Study of Oral Literature, 1978.

_____. "Themes of the Young Hero in Serbocroatian Oral Epic Tradition." *PMLA* 83 (1968):1296–1303.

Campbell, E. F. *Ruth*. Anchor Bible. Garden City, NJ: Doubleday, 1975.

Campbell, Joseph. *The Hero with a Thousand Faces*. Bollingen Series, vol. 17. Princeton: Princeton University, 1949.

Cazelles, Henri. "*Notes sur las composition du rouleau d'Esther.*" In *Lex tua veritas: Festschrift für Hubert Junker*, ed. Heinrich Gross and Franz Mussner. Trier: Paulinas, 1961.

Child, F. J. *English and Scottish Popular Ballads*. 5 vols. Boston: Houghton Mifflin, 1882–1890.

Christiansen, R. Th. *Norske Eventyr*. Den Norske Historiske Kildeskriftkommission. Kristiania: Jacob Dybwad, 1921.

Coats, George W. *From Canaan to Egypt: Structural and Theological Context for the Joseph Story*. CBQMS no. 4. Washington: Catholic Biblical Association, 1976.

Cook, V. "Lord Raglan's Hero—A Cross-Cultural Critique." *Florida Anthropologist* 18 (1964):147–54.

Coote, Robert. "The Application of Oral Theory to Biblical Hebrew Literature." *Semeia* 5 (1976):51–64.

_____. "Tradition, Oral, OT." In *IDB* Supp. 914–16.

Cox, Patricia. *Biography in Late Antiquity: A Quest for the Holy Man.* Berkeley and Los Angeles: University of California Press, 1983.

Cross, F. M. "The Epic Traditions of Early Israel: Epic Narrative and the Reconstruction of Early Israelite Institutions." In *The Poet and the Historian: Essays in Literary and Historical Biblical Criticism,* ed. R. E. Friedman, 13–39. Harvard Semitic Studies 26. Chico, CA: Scholars, 1983.

Culley, Robert C. *Oral Formulaic Language in the Biblical Psalms.* Near and Middle East Series 4. Toronto: University of Toronto Press, 1967.

_____. "Oral Tradition and Historicity." In *Studies on the Ancient Palestinian World,* ed. J. Wevers and D. B. Redford, 102–16. Toronto: University of Toronto Press, 1972.

_____. "Oral Tradition and the OT: Some Recent Discussion." *Semeia* 5 (1976):1–33.

_____. "Punishment Stories in the Legends of the Prophets." In *Orientation by Disorientation: Studies in Literary Criticism Presented in Honor of William A. Beardslee,* ed. Richard A. Spenser, 167–81. Pittsburgh Theological Monograph Ser. 35. Pittsburgh: Pickwick, 1980.

_____. "Structural Analysis: Is It Done with Mirrors?" *Interpretation* 28 (1974):165–81.

_____. *Studies in the Structure of Hebrew Narrative. Semeia* Supp. Missoula, MT, and Philadelphia: Scholars and Fortress, 1976.

_____. "Themes and Variations in Three Groups of Old Testament Narratives." *Semeia* 3 (1975):3–13.

_____, ed. *Oral Tradition and Old Testament Studies. Semeia* 5 (1976).

Culley, Robert C., and Thomas W. Overholt. *Anthropological Perspectives on Old Testament Prophecy. Semeia* 21 (1981).

Daube, David. *Collaboration with Tyranny in Rabbinic Law.* The Riddell Memorial Lectures, 1965. London: Oxford University Press, 1965.

Degh, Linda, and Andrew Vazsonyi. "The Hypothesis of Multi-Conduit Transmission in Folklore." In *Folklore: Performance and Communication,* 207–52. *See* Ben-Amos and Goldstein.

Dorson, Richard. *Folklore and Folklife.* Chicago: University of Chicago Press, 1972.

————. *Folklore: Selected Essays.* Bloomington: Indiana University Press, 1972.

————, ed. *Folklore and Traditional History.* The Hague: Mouton, 1973.

Douglas, Mary. *Purity and Danger.* New York: Praeger, 1966.

Drake, Carlos C. "Jung and His Critics." *JAF* 80 (1967):321–33.

————. "Jungian Psychology and Its Use in Folklore." *JAF* 82 (1969):122–31.

Dundes, Alan. *Analytic Essays in Folklore.* The Hague and Paris: Mouton, 1975.

————. "From Etic to Emic Units in the Structural Study of Folktales." In *Analytic Essays in Folklore,* 61–72.

————. "The Hero Pattern and the Life of Jesus." In *Interpreting Folklore,* 223–61.

————. *Interpreting Folklore.* Bloomington: Indiana University Press, 1980.

————. "The Making and Breaking of a Friendship as a Structural Frame in African Folk Tales." In *Structural Analysis of Oral Tradition,* ed. Pierre Maranda and Elli Köngäs Maranda. Philadelphia: University of Pennsylvania Press, 1971.

————. *The Morphology of North American Indian Tales.* FFC 195. Helsinki: Suomalainen tiedeakatemia, 1965.

————. "On the Structure of the Proverb," *Proverbium* 25 (1975):961–73.

————. "Structural Typology in North American Indian Folktales." In *The Study of Folklore,* 206–15.

————. " 'To Love My Father All': A Psychoanalytic Study of the Folktale Source of *King Lear.*" In *Cinderella: A Folktale Casebook,* 229–44.

Dundes, Alan, ed. *Cinderella: A Folktale Casebook.* New York: Garland, 1982.

————, ed. *Sacred Narrative.* Berkeley and Los Angeles: University of California Press, 1984.

————, ed. *The Study of Folklore.* Englewood Cliffs, NJ: Prentice-Hall, 1965.

Edwards, Jay D. *The Afro-American Trickster Tale: A Structural Analysis.* Monograph Series of the Folklore Publications Group 4. Bloomington: Indiana University Press, 1978.

Eliade, Mircea. *Shamanism.* Bollingen Series, vol. 76. Princeton: Princeton University Press, 1972.

Emerton, J. A. "An Examination of a Recent Structuralist Interpretation of Genesis XXXVIII." *VT* (1976):79–98.

Evans-Pritchard, E. E. *The Zande Trickster.* Oxford: Clarendon, 1967.

Finnegan, Ruth. "A Note on Oral Tradition and Historical Evidence." *History and Theory* 9 (1970):195–201.

Fishbane, Michael. *Text and Texture*. New York: Schocken, 1979.

Fokkelman, J. P. *Narrative Art in Genesis*. Amsterdam: Van Gorcum, 1975.

Foley, John Miles. *Oral-Formulaic Theory and Research: An Introduction and Annotated Bibliography*. New York: Garland, 1985.

_____. *Oral Tradition in Literature*. Columbia: University of Missouri Press, 1986.

Fontaine, Carole R. *Traditional Sayings in the Old Testament*. Sheffield: Almond, 1982.

Freilich, Morris. "Lévi-Strauss' Myth of Method." In *Patterns in Oral Literature*, 223–49. See Jason and Segal.

Gan, M. "The Book of Esther in the Light of Joseph's Fate in Egypt." (Hebrew) *Tarbiz* 31 (1962):144–49.

Gaster, Theodor H. *Purim and Hanukkah in Custom and Tradition*. New York: Schuman, 1950.

Geertz, Clifford. *The Interpretation of Cultures*. New York: Basic, 1974.

_____. "Religion as a Cultural System." In *The Interpretation of Cultures*, 87–125. New York: Basic, 1974.

Gendler, Mary. "The Restoration of Vashti." In *The Jewish Women*, ed. Elizabeth Koltun. New York: Schocken, 1976.

Georges, Robert A. and Alan Dundes. "Toward a Structural Definition of the Riddle." In *Analytic Essays in Folklore*, 95–102. See Dundes.

Gerleman, G. *Esther*. BKAT 21. Neukirchen-Vluyn: Neukirchener Verlag, 1973.

_____. *Studien zu Esther; Stoff-Structure-Stil-Sinn*. Neukirchen-Vluyn: Neukirchener Verlag, 1966.

Gevirtz, Stanley. *Patterns in the Early Poetry of Israel*. Studies in Ancient Oriental Civilization 32. Chicago: University of Chicago Press, 1963.

Gottwald, Norman. *The Tribes of Yahweh: A Sociology of the Religion of Liberated Israel 1250–1050 B.C.* Maryknoll, NY: Orbis, 1979.

Greenberg, Moshe. "Rabbinic Reflections on Defying Illegal Orders: Amasa, Abner, and Joab." In *Contemporary Jewish Ethics*, ed. M. M. Kellner. New York: Sanhedrin, 1978.

Greengus, S. "Sisterhood Adoption at Nuzi and the 'Wife-Sister' in Genesis." *HUCA* 46 (1975):5–31.

Greimas, Algirdas Julien. "*Le Conte populaire russe (analyse fonctionnelle)*." *International Journal of Slavic Linguistics and Poetics* 9 (1965):152–75.

————. "The Interpretation of Myth: Theory and Practice." In *Structural Analysis of Oral Tradition*, 81–121. *See* Maranda and Maranda.

————. *Sémantique structurale*. Paris: Lacouse, 1966.

Gunkel, Hermann. *Esther*. Religionsgeschichtliche Volksbucher. II Reihe. 19/20. Tübingen: J. C. B. Mohr, 1916.

————. *Genesis*. Göttingen: Vandenhoeck and Ruprecht, 1910.

————. "Jakob." *Preussische Jahrbucher* 176, 3 (1919):339–62.

————. "*Die Komposition der Joseph-Geschichten*." ZDMG 76 (1922):55–71.

————. *Legends of Genesis*. New York: Schocken, 1966.

————. *Das Märchen im alten Testament*. Religionsgeschichtliche Volksbucher. II Reihe. 23/26. Tübingen: J. C. B. Mohr, 1917, 1921.

Gunn, David. "Narrative Patterns and Oral Tradition in Judges and Samuel." *VT* 24 (1974):286–317.

————. "Traditional Narrative Composition in the 'Succession Narrative.'" *VT* 26 (1976):214–29.

Hahn, J. G. von. *Sagwissenschaftliche Studien*. Jena: Friedrich Mauke, 1876.

Haymes, Edward R. *A Bibliography of Studies Relating to Parry's and Lord's Oral Theory*. Cambridge: Center for the Study of Oral Literature, Harvard University, 1973.

Hendel, Ronald. "The Epic of the Patriarch: The Jacob Cycle and the Narrative Traditions of Canaan and Israel." Ph.D. diss., Harvard University, 1985.

Horn, S. "Mordecai, A Historical Problem." *BR* 9 (1964):14–25.

Humphreys, W. Lee. "A Life-style for Diaspora: A Study of the Tales of Esther and Daniel." *JBL* 93 (1973):211–23.

Hymes, Del. "Breakthrough into Performance." In *Folklore: Performance and Communication*, 11–74. *See* Ben-Amos and Goldstein.

Irvin, Dorothy. "The Joseph and Moses Stories as Narrative in the Light of Ancient Near Eastern Narrative." In *Israelite and Judaean History*, ed. J. H. Hayes and J. M. Miller, 180–209. Philadelphia: Westminster, 1977.

————. *Mytharion: The Comparison of Tales from the Old Testament and the Ancient Near East*. Veroffentlichungen zur Kultur und Geschichte des Alten Testaments vol. 32. Neukirchen-Vluyn: Neukirchener Verlag, 1978.

Jason, Heda, and Dimitri Segal, eds. *Patterns in Oral Literature*. The Hague and Paris: Mouton, 1977.

————. "The Problem of 'Tale Role' and 'Character' in Propp's Work." In *Patterns in Oral Literature*. *See* Jason and Segal.

Jobling, David. *The Sense of Biblical Narrative: Three Structural Analyses in the Old Testament*. *JSOT* Supp. vol. 7. Sheffield: Almond, 1973.

Jolles, André. *Einfache Formen*. Halle: Niemeyer, 1929.

Jones, Bruce W. "Two Misconceptions about the Book of Esther." *CBQ* 39 (1977):171-81.

Kelber, Werner. *The Oral and the Written Gospel*. Philadelphia: Fortress, 1983.

Keller, Carl A. *"Die Gefährdung der Anfrau."* *ZAW* (1955):181-91.

Kirshenblatt-Gimblett, Barbara. "Culture Shock and Narrative Creativity." In *Folklore in the Modern World*, ed. Richard M. Dorson, 109-22. The Hague and Paris: Mouton, 1978.

_____. "A Parable in Context: A Social Interactional Analysis of Storytelling Performance." In *Folklore: Performance and Communication*, 105-30. See Ben-Amos and Goldstein.

Knowles, J. H. *Folk-Tales of Kashmir*. London: Kegan, Paul, Trench, Trubner, 1893.

Koch, Klaus. *The Growth of the Biblical Tradition*. London: Adam and Charles Black, 1969.

Kselman, John R. "The Recovery of Poetic Fragments from the Pentateuchal Priestly Source." *JBL* 97 (1978):161-73.

Kugel, James A. *The Idea of Biblical Poetry: Parallelism and Its History*. New Haven: Yale University, 1981.

Leach, Edmond. *Genesis As Myth and Other Essays*. London: Jonathan Cape, 1969.

Leach, MacEdward. *The Ballad Book*. New York: A. S. Barnes, 1955.

Lebram, J. C. H. *"Purimfest und Estherbuch."* *VT* 22 (1972):208-22.

Lévi Strauss, Claude. *Structural Anthropology*. New York: Harper & Row, 1970.

_____. "The Structural Study of Myth." In *Myth. A Symposium*, ed. Thomas A. Sebeok, 81-95. Bloomington: Indiana University, 1958.

Long, Burke O. "The Social Function of Conflict Among the Prophets." In *Anthropological Perspectives on Old Testament Prophecy*, 31-53. See Culley and Overholt.

Lord, A. B. "The Gospels As Oral Traditional Literature." In *The Relationship among the Gospels: An Interdisciplinary Dialogue*, ed. William O. Walker, Jr., 33-91. San Antonio, TX: Trinity University Press, 1978.

_____. "History and Tradition in Balkan Oral Epic and Ballad," *Western Folklore* 31 (1972):53-60.

_____. *The Singer of Tales*. New York: Atheneum, 1968.

Lowth, Robert. "Lecture XIX." In *Lectures on the Sacred Poetry of the Hebrews*, trans. G. Gregory, A New Edition with notes by Calvin E. Stowe, 154–66. Boston: Crocker & Brewster, 1929.

Lundell, Torborg. "Making Mother Conform to Standards." In Program and Abstracts, Annual Meeting, AFS, 1985, 50–51.

Lüthi, Max. "Aspects of the *Märchen* and the Legend." In *Folklore Genres*, 17–33. See Ben-Amos.

————. *The European Folktale: Form and Nature*. Trans. John D. Niles. Philadelphia: ISHI, 1982.

MacDonald, Dennis R. *The Legend and the Apostle: The Battle for Paul in Story and Canon*. Philadelphia: Westminster, 1983.

McKane, William. *Studies in the Patriarchal Narratives*. Edinburgh: Handsel, 1979.

Maly, E. "Genesis 12, 10–20; 20, 1–18; 26, 7–11 and the Pentateuchal Question." *CBQ* 18 (1956):255–62.

Maranda, Elli-Kaija Köngäs. "The Concept of Folklore." *Midwest Folklore* 13 (1963):69–88.

Maranda, Elli Köngäs, and Maranda, Pierre. *Structural Models in Folklore and Transformational Essays*. Approaches to Semiotics vol. 10. The Hague and Paris: Mouton, 1971.

Mark, Vera. "Images of Women in Gascon Verbal Art." In Program and Abstracts, Annual Meeting, AFS, 1985, 51–52.

Meinhold, Arndt. "*Die Gattung der Josephsgeschichte und des Esterbuches: Diasporanovelle I.*" *ZAW* 87 (1975):306–24.

————. "*Dia Gattung der Josephsgeschichte und des Esterbuches: Diasporanovelle II.*" *ZAW* 88 (1976):72–93.

Mendenhall, George. *The Tenth Generation*. Baltimore: Johns Hopkins, 1973.

Merez, Herminia Q. "Filipino-American Erotica and the Ethnography of a Folkloric Event." In *Folklore: Performance and Communication*, 131–41. See Ben-Amos and Goldstein.

Mills, Margaret. "Afghan Popular Romances and Creative Consciousness." In Program and Abstracts, Annual Meeting, AFS, 1985, 54.

Milne, Pamela. "Folktales and Fairy Tales: An Evaluation of Two Proppian Analyses of Biblical Narrative." *JSOT* 34 (1986):35–60.

Miscall, Peter. "The Jacob and Joseph Stories as Analogies." *JSOT* 6 (1978):28–40.

Momigliano, Arnaldo. *The Development of Greek Biography*. Cambridge: Harvard University Press, 1971.

Moore, Carey A. *Esther*. Anchor Bible. Garden City, NJ: Doubleday, 1971.

Neumann, Erich. *The Origins and History of Consciousness*. Bollingen Series, vol. 42. New York: Pantheon, 1954.

Niditch, Susan. *Chaos to Cosmos: Studies in Biblical Patterns of Creation*. Chico, CA: Scholars, 1984.

⸻. "The Composition of Isaiah 1." *Biblica* 61 (1980):509–29.

⸻. "Legends of Wise Heroes and Heroines." In *The Hebrew Bible and Its Modern Interpreters*, ed. D. Knight and G. Tucker, 445–63. Chico, CA: Scholars, 1985.

⸻. *The Symbolic Vision in Biblical Tradition*. Chico, CA: Scholars, 1980.

⸻. "The Visionary." In *Ideal Figures in Ancient Judaism*, ed. John J. Collins and George W. E. Nickelsburg, 153–79. Septuagint and Cognate Studies vol. 12. Chico, CA: Scholars, 1980.

⸻. "The Wronged Woman Righted: An Analysis of Genesis 38." *HTR* 72 (1979):143–49.

Niditch, Susan, and Robert Doran. "The Success Story of the Wise Courtier." *JBL* 96 (1977):179–93.

Oden, Robert. "Divine Aspirations in Atrahasis and in Genesis 1–11." *ZAW* 93 (1981):197–216.

⸻. "Jacob as Father, Husband, and Nephew: Kinship Studies and the Patriarchal Narratives." *JBL* 102 (1983):189–205.

⸻. "Transformations in Near Eastern Myths." *Religion* 11 (1981):21–37.

Olrik, Axel. "Epic Laws of Folk Narrative." In *The Study of Folklore*, 131–41. See Dundes.

Oppenheim, A. Leo. *The Interpretation of Dreams in the Ancient Near East TAPA* 46/3 (1956).

Pace, David. "Beyond Morphology: Lévi-Strauss and the Analysis of Folktales." In *Cinderella: A Folktale Casebook*, 245–58. See Dundes.

Patte, Daniel, ed. *Genesis 2 and 3: Kaleidoscopic Structural Readings*. *Semeia* 18 (1960).

Pelton, Robert. *The Trickster in West Africa*. Berkeley and Los Angeles: University of California Press, 1980.

Pike, Kenneth L. *Language in Relation to a Unified Theory of the Structure of Behavior*. Part 1. Glendale, CA: Summer Institute of Linguistics, 1954–1960.

Polzin, Robert. "The Ancestress of Israel in Danger." *Semeia* 3 (1975):81–98.

_____. *Biblical Structuralism: Method and Subjectivity in the Study of Ancient Texts*. Missoula, MT: Scholars, 1977.

Propp, Vladimir. *The Morphology of the Folktale*. Austin: University of Texas Press, 1960.

_____. *Theory and History of Folktale*. Trans. A. Martin and R. Martin. Ed. A. Liberman. Theory and History of Literature vol. 5. Minneapolis: University of Minnesota Press, 1984.

Pury, Albert de. *Promesse divine et légende cultuelle dans le cycle de Jacob*. 2 vols. Études Bibliques. Paris: Gabalda, 1975.

Rad, Gerhard von. *Genesis*. Philadelphia: Westminster, 1961.

_____. "The Joseph Narrative and Ancient Wisdom." In *The Problem of the Hexateuch and Other Essays*. New York: McGraw Hill, 1966.

_____. *Die Josephsgeschichte*. B St vol. 5. Neukirchen-Vluyn: Neukirchener Verlag, 1959.

Radin, Paul. "The Religion of the North American Indians." *Journal of the American Folklore Society* 27 (1914):335-73.

_____. *The Trickster*. New York: Philosophical Library, 1956.

Raglan, Lord. *The Hero*. New York: Vintage, 1956.

Rank, Otto. "The Myth of the Birth of the Hero." In *Myth of the Birth of the Hero and Other Writings by Otto Rank*, ed. Philip Freund. New York: Vintage, 1964.

Redford, Donald. *A Study of the Biblical Story of Joseph, Genesis 37-50*. VT Supp. vol. 20. Leiden: Brill, 1970.

Ricketts, MacLinscott. "The North American Indian Trickster." *HR* 5 (1965):327-50.

_____. "The Structure and Religious Significance of the Trickster–Transformer–Culture Hero in the Mythology of the North American Indians." Ph.D. diss., University of Chicago, 1964.

Rivers, W. H. R. "The Sociological Significance of Myth." In *Studies on Mythology*, ed. R. A. Georges, 27-45. Homewood, IL: Dorsey, 1968.

Rosenthal, L. A. "*Die Josephsgeschichte mit den Buchem Ester und Daniel verglichen*." *ZAW* 15 (1895):278-84.

_____. "*Nochmals der Vergleich Ester-Joseph*." *ZAW* 17 (1897):126-28.

Ross, Rita. "The Forbidden Chamber." In Program and Abstracts, Annual Meeting, AFS, 1985, 61.

Rubenstein, Ben. "The Meaning of the Cinderella Story in the Development of a Little Girl." In *Cinderella: A Folktale Casebook*, 219-28. See Dundes.

Sandmel, Samuel. "The Haggada within Scripture." *JBL* 80 (1961):105-22.

————. *The Hebrew Scriptures: An Introduction to Their Literature and Religious Ideas.* New York: Oxford University Press, 1978.

Sasson, J. M. *Ruth: A Translation with a Philological Commentary and a Formalist-Folklorist Interpretation.* Baltimore: Johns Hopkins Press, 1979.

Schedl, Claus. *"Das Buch Esther." Theologie und Gegenwart* (1964):85–93.

Schmidt, D. Hans, and Paul Kahle. *Volkserzählungen aus Palästina.* 2 vols. Göttingen: Vandenhoeck und Ruprecht, 1918, 1930.

Selbman, Rolf. *Der deutsche Bildungsroman.* Stuttgart: Metzlersche, 1984.

Speiser, E. A. *Genesis.* Anchor Bible. Garden City, NJ: Doubleday, 1964.

————. "The Wife-Sister Motif in the Patriarchal Narratives." In *Oriental and Biblical Studies,* ed. J. J. Finkelstein and M. Greenberg. Philadelphia: University of Pennsylvania Press, 1969.

Strutynski, Udo. "The Survival of Indo-European Mythology in Germanic Legendry." *JAF* 97 (1984):43–56.

Swales, Martin. *The German Bildungsroman from Wieland to Hesse.* Princeton: Princeton University Press, 1978.

Sydow, Carl Wilhelm von. *"Kategorien der Prosa-Volksdichtung."* In *Selected Papers on Folklore,* ed. Laurits Bødker, 60–88. Copenhagen: Rosenkilde & Bagger, 1984.

————. "Popular Prose Traditions and Their Classification." In *Selected Papers on Folklore,* 127–45.

Talmon, Shemaryahu. "Wisdom in the Book of Esther." *VT* 13 (1963):419–55.

Thompson, Stith. *The Folktale.* New York: Holt, Reinhart & Winston, 1946.

————. *The Motif-Index of Folk-Literature.* Bloomington: Indiana University Press, 1955–1958.

————. "The Star Husband Tale." In *The Study of Folklore,* 414–74. See Dundes.

————, ed. and trans. *The Types of the Folktale.* FFC 184. Helsinki: Suomalainen tiedeakatemia, 1973 (an expanded edition of Antti Aarne's *Verzeichnis der Märchentypen*).

Thompson, Thomas L. "Conflict of Themes in the Jacob Narrative." *Semeia* 15 (1979):5–26.

Tigay, Jeffrey. *The Evolution of the Gilgamesh Epic.* Philadelphia: University of Pennsylvania Press, 1982.

Todorov, Tzvetan. *Théorie de la littérature.* Paris: Édition du seuil, 1965.

Toelken, Barre. *The Dynamics of Folklore.* Boston: Houghton Mifflin, 1979.

Turner, Victor. *Dramas, Fields, and Metaphors: Symbolic Action in Human Society.* Ithaca: Cornell University Press, 1974.

———. *The Ritual Process.* Ithaca: Cornell University Press, 1969.

Ungnad, A. "Keilinscriftliche Beiträge zum Buch Ezra und Esther." *ZAW* 58 (1964):20–24.

Urbrock, William J. "Evidences of Oral-Formulaic Composition in the Poetry of Job." Ph.D. diss., Harvard University, 1975.

Utley, Frances Lee. "Folk Literature: An Operational Definition." In *The Study of Folklore*, 7–24. See Dundes.

Van Seters, John. *Abraham in History and Tradition.* New Haven: Yale University Press, 1975.

Vansina, Jan. *Oral Tradition. A Study in Historical Methodology.* Chicago: Aldine, 1965.

Walker, Warren S., and Ahmet E. Uysal. *Tales Alive in Turkey.* Cambridge: Harvard University Press, 1966.

Wescott, Joan. "The Sculpture and Myths of Eshu-Elegba, the Yoruba Trickster: Definition and Interpretation in Yoruba Iconography." *Africa* (Journal of the International African Institute) 32 (1966):336–53.

Westermann, Claus. *The Promises to the Fathers.* Philadelphia: Fortress, 1980.

Whallon, William. *Formula, Character, and Context.* Publications of the Center for Hellenic Studies. Cambridge: Harvard University, 1969.

Wilcoxen, Jay A. "Narrative." In *Old Testament Form Criticism*, ed. John H. Hayes, 57–98. San Antonio: Trinity University Press, 1974.

Williams, James G. "The Beautiful and the Barren: Conventions in Biblical Type-Scenes." *JSOT* 17 (1980):107–19.

Wilson, Pamela. "Keeping the Record Straight: The Social Function of Gossip." In Program and Abstracts, Annual Meeting, AFS, 1985, 69.

Wilson, Robert R. *Genealogy and History in the Biblical World.* New Haven: Yale University Press, 1977.

———. *Prophecy and Society in Ancient Israel.* Philadelphia: Fortress, 1980.

Wittig, Susan. "Theories of Formulaic Narrative." *Semeia* 15 (1976):65–91.

Yoder, Perry Bruce. "A-B Pairs and Oral Composition in Hebrew Poetry." *VT* 21 (1971):470–89.

General Index

Scripture Index